MW01223614

Leadership
& Conflict

Creative Leadership Series

Leadership & Conflict

Speed B. Leas

Creative Leadership Series
Lyle E. Schaller, Editor

Abingdon Press/Nashville

Leadership and Conflict

Copyright © 1982 by Abingdon Press

Eighth Printing 1992

All rights reserved.

This book is printed on recycled, acid-free paper.

Library of Congress Cataloging-in-Publication Data

LEAS, SPEED, 1937-
  Leadership and conflict.
  (Creative leadership series)
  1. Leadership. 2. Organizational behavior.
  I. Title. II. Series.
  BF637.L4L43   158'.4   82-6788   AACR2

ISBN 0-687-21264-2

The selection on page 18 is from the article "Debating the Unknowable" by Lewis Thomas, published in *The Atlantic Monthly*, July 1981. Reprinted by permission of Harold Ober Associates Incorporated. Copyright © 1981 by Lewis Thomas.

The quotation on pages 36-37 is from the article "Good Guys Make Bum Bosses" by David C. McClelland and David H. Burnham, December 1975. Reprinted from *Psychology Today* magazine. Copyright © 1975 Ziff Davis Publishing Co. Used by permission.

The chart on page 39 is from the article "Leadership and Organizational Excitement" by David Berlew, published in *The California Management Review* by the University of California, Berkeley.

Quotations on pages 51, 52, and 54 are from *From Panic to Power* by John Parrino. Used by permission of John Wiley & Sons, Inc., publishers.

The list of pages 56-57 is from the book *A New Guide to Rational Living* by Albert Ellis and Robert A. Harper. © 1975 by Institute for Rational Living, Inc. Published by Prentice-Hall, Inc. Used by permission.

The lists on pages 70-71, and 72 are from *The Relationship Manual* by David Luecke. Used by permission of The Relationship Institute, 10751 Evening Wind Court, Columbia, Maryland 21044.

MANUFACTURED IN THE UNITED STATES OF AMERICA

This book is dedicated to:
Bob Beeching
Bruce MacKenzie
Henry Hayden
Nick Piedescalzi
Four leaders from whom I learned what it
means to be a mature human being and about
healthy voluntary systems

Foreword

Conflict may be the most widespread inhibiting factor in Western society today. Every business leader recognizes that internal conflict is inhibiting the progress of that organization. Governmental leaders realize that the conflicts over goals and priorities between subordinates and among the employees reduces productivity. The principal of the local high school spends many hours every month attempting to resolve conflict. On any given day in perhaps three-quarters of all churches the ministry of that congregation is reduced significantly as a result of nonproductive conflict. In perhaps one-fourth of all churches that internal conflict is so sufficiently severe that it must be reduced before the parish can redirect its energies and resources toward formulating new goals and expanding its ministry.

When asked about desired improvements in their leadership skills, a substantial majority of business executives, educational leaders, governmental officials, pastors, military officers, labor leaders, denominational executives, and volunteers in community organizations lift up skills in conflict management as a high priority.

While some will argue that leadership is a gift of God-given talent, not a skill, Speed Leas makes it very clear in this volume that *skills* in conflict resolution can be identified, taught, and learned. He does that here.

Leaders from all facets of the culture will find that this

volume speaks to their basic concerns as leaders, and from within that context the author offers helpful insights and suggestions on the creative management of conflict.

This is one of several volumes in the Creative Leadership Series that has been designed to reach a broad audience of persons who carry significant leadership responsibilities every day of the week. Those who appreciate the insights and help they receive from this book may want to turn to other volumes in the series including one on enlisting volunteers by Douglas W. Johnson, the earlier book on time management by Speed B. Leas, and one on leading people in planned change by Douglas Alan Walrath.

Lyle E. Schaller
Yokefellow Institute
Richmond, Indiana

Contents

Introduction

I was teaching a course in conflict management for a group of leaders in Toronto and thought I was doing very well from the response I was getting until Larry Peterson sat down next to me at lunch. "You want some feedback?" he asked.

"Sure," I replied, expecting to hear that I didn't make the breaks long enough or that the instructions for the conflict exercise were not clear to his group.

"I think you're misleading us by calling this course 'conflict management,' " he declared. "When a young man from the community action agency said he got fired from his last job because he refused to run personal errands for his boss, you said, 'Well, you can't win 'em all,' and when the woman who was appointed to the planning commission complained about the continuous disruptive behavior of her fellow board members, you indicated that might have been a situation where she should consider resigning from the board. The word 'management' implies that you can control the situation, but in both of those instances it was clear that those people were unable to control anything, and they were getting a raw deal."

"I think you have a good point, Larry," I responded. "Sometimes the word 'management' implies overseeing, directing, controlling, and one hopes when coming to a conflict management course that never again will bullies kick sand in your face. I have avoided using the word conflict resolution because it implies that you can 'fix' every fight that you get into, and we all know that's not possible. I use the word 'management' in the sense used by a skier who was having his broken leg set and was asked how he was going to get to the office on Monday. He replied, 'I haven't figured that out yet, but I'll *manage* somehow.' In his case, to 'manage' means to 'get along' or 'make out' or 'muddle through.' So perhaps the course should be called 'doing the best you can under the circumstances.' "

Larry brought me to an awareness that much of what I had read and taught over the past fifteen years in the field of conflict and leadership implied that if you do it right, you can win, stay cool and collected, and amaze your friends and relatives by knowing exactly what to do no matter what happens. That is not what I intend to say to you in this book. Rather, I will describe what research and experience have shown to be useful in helping organizations and individuals deal with differences and conflict. No guarantees or magic answers will be found here.

Frankly, there is little science of leadership or science of conflict management such as in the mathematical sciences where there is a body of truths systematically arranged, showing the operation of general laws. In conflict management each area is connected with a body of knowledge, an abundance of advice coming from sage experience, a plethora of commonly agreed-on rules or norms that shape understanding of what is fair, and research on some of the factors that escalate and de-escalate controversy.

In this book I will draw on the science that exists, on the experiences of others that have been proven helpful, and on my own experience as a consultant to organizations in conflict.

As I write, I have a particular audience in mind. I am writing to those who consider themselves to have leadership skills and responsibilities in organized community, business, religious, and government settings. When I say leadership skills and responsibilities in these organizations, I do not mean exclusively the formally elected or appointed leaders (though certainly this book is written for those who are). I also mean those who influence the direction of a group and the participation of its members, though they may not be the officially elected or appointed leaders.

This book is not written to cover all leadership situations, only those in which conflict is or should be a part of the picture. These are the times when the group gets bogged down in attacking and blaming, bickering, spreading rumors, or painfully struggling with differences of values or goals between people who care about the good of the group and also care very much about their own priorities. I assume that not all cases of conflict and difference need to be de–escalated. There are times when too little conflict is apparent in the organization, and in order to awaken the group or to deal with important issues that people are burying, actions should be taken that will surface underlying difference.

I am further assuming that as a leader you will find yourself in a variety of conflict situations at different stages in your organization's life. Sometimes de-escalation and conflict suppression will be your highest priority; at other times advocacy or surfacing the differences will be needed.

In the first chapter you will find the development of a theory of human needs which will lay the foundation for the material that follows. The second and third chapters focus on a general theory of leadership, followed by the fourth chapter on the effect of fear on conflict dynamics. After the first four chapters, which are more general, you will find specific helps for certain conflict situations: surfacing submerged conflict, dealing with the organization as a system and its environment, curbing or reducing conflict, advocacy, and self-defense.

I wish to acknowledge here my appreciation of colleagues, mentors, and friends who have contributed greatly to my understanding of leadership and conflict and who have graciously read and critiqued this manuscript. Especially helpful to this project have been Loren Mead, Elaine Gaston, Ruth Wright, Nancy Geyer, and Rod Reinecke. My thanks also to Carol Cunningham who has worked with me for five years as a superb administrative assistant and secretary. Carol has contributed greatly to the production of this manuscript and to the work that I do as a consultant.

Speed B. Leas
The Alban Institute

I

Leadership and Subordinancy

As every person who has been in leadership knows, the experience is often accompanied by a perplexing equivocal behavior from those who relate to the leader. One day you think you are a part of a loyal, collaborative company and the next you find yourself with a renegade who has turned against your leadership. What did you do to provoke this turncoat behavior? Perhaps nothing. Often, conflict with leaders comes from the healthy, yet annoying needs of followers to express their own individuality by challenging the head of the group. This is not only a problem for leaders but also a problem for members.

I can illustrate this common human experience of "insubordination." Some years ago Connie, my wife, and I took a trip down the Stanislaus River in California. The Stanislaus is a white-water river which can only be rafted by rubber boat. To make the trip it is necessary to pay an outfitter who provides the rafts, meals, oarsmen, and other necessities for the trip. Connie and I rode in the raft with Tony, who owned the equipment, organized the trips, and hired the crew. He was indeed an experienced captain. He had been traveling this river every spring and summer for the past nine years. He was bronzed from the sun, muscled from steering the boats, and charmingly knowledgeable about the river: its history, water, rocks, flora, and fauna.

To say the least, I felt safe and excited to be with Tony. He was the boss; he was an experienced oarsman; and he clearly was the most informed about the river. I listened to everything he had to say and was impressed. When Tony asked me to do something, in order to be accommodating to him and the others, I jumped at the chance. If he needed help unloading the boat, I was right there. If he wanted to know about rocks or other boats up ahead, I was the first to call back a response.

At one point on the river a particular chute of water raced between two rocks. Tony said it was great fun to jump out of the boat and let the water carry you through. Though we had heard many stories of careless boaters who had lost their lives in certain rapids upstream, Tony's assurance that this was a safe place to jump in and be carried through the chute was encouragement enough for me. With little hesitation I dove in and was whipped through the channel in an exhilarating and exciting ride. At the bottom of the run of water, Tony and the others picked me up.

At the end of the day, Connie and I talked about the great adventure we had had. Tony had done all the thinking and preparation for us. He led us through new, exciting experiences and his demeanor and assurance led me to believe that, though there was real risk, I was safe if I followed his advice and example. He also helped us discover a wonderful new place.

We were so "turned on" by this experience that we convinced some friends to go on the same trip with us the next summer. They agreed to go, and I called Tony to make reservations—specifying we wanted to be sure to be in his boat on this second trip. We hadn't been on the river half an hour before I recognized that Tony was

16

telling the same stories, the same jokes, and doing things exactly as he had done on our first trip. Somehow, I had lost the excitement I had on the earlier trip, and I was annoyed at Tony; for what, I wasn't sure.

Presently, I found myself telling our friends Tony's stories before we got to the appropriate place on the river. I told them it wouldn't be long before we came to "Deadman's Rapids" where an inexperienced rafter lost his life trying to run the rapids after a thunderstorm. I told them about the mining camp we would be coming to and approximately how much gold was taken out of the river each day. When it came time to have lunch, I felt that Tony was not distributing the food properly, nor was he giving us enough time to explore the area where we had stopped. I then got into an argument with him about whether we should start down the river or wait another half hour until we had digested our lunch.

This emerging conflict between Tony and me illustrates the antagonistic proclivities for cooperation or subordinancy on the one hand and independence on the other that make leadership possible and conflict inevitable. On the earlier trip I did not let myself be aware of my needs for control and leadership when I perceived my survival and my good time was dependent on learning from Tony how rafting is done. However, as my confidence increased, I began to let myself be aware of other needs which I had submerged or didn't allow myself to recognize before.

The Need to Cooperate

Like all social animals, human beings have a mechanism or a need that leads them to band together in joint

17

ventures for the good of the species as well as for the good of the individual. As I think about these predilections, I am reminded of the writing of Lewis Thomas and his reflections on interdependence:

> There is a . . . phenomenon in entomology known as stigmergy, a term invented by Grasse, which means "to incite to work." When three or four termites are collected together in a chamber they wander about aimlessly, but when more termites are added, they begin to build. It is the presence of other termites, in sufficient numbers at close quarters, that produces the work: they pick up each other's fecal pellets and stack them in neat columns, and when the columns are precisely the right height, the termites reach across and turn the perfect arches that form the foundation of the termination. No single termite knows how to do any of this, but as soon as there are enough termites gathered together they become flawless architects, sensing their distances from each other although blind, building an immensely complicated structure with its own air-conditioning and humidity control. They work their lives away in this ecosystem built by themselves.

One of the keynotes of all of Thomas' work is that there is a tendency for living things to join up whenever joining is possible: accommodation and compromise are more common results of close contact than combat and destruction. He notes this phenomena across species lines as well as within species. He describes social animals in this way:

> Not all social animals are social with the same degree of commitment. In some species, the members are so tied to each other and interdependent as to seem the loosely conjoined cells of a tissue. The social insects are like this; they move, and live all their lives, in a mass; a beehive is a spherical animal. In other species, less compulsively

social, the members make their homes together, pool resources, travel in packs or schools, and share the food, but any single one can survive solitary, detached from the rest. Others are social only in the sense of being more or less congenial, meeting from time to time in committees, using social gatherings as *ad hoc* occasions for feeding and breeding. Some animals simply nod at each other in passing, never reaching even a first-name relationship. . . . Social animals tend to keep at a particular thing, generally something huge for their size; they work at it ceaselessly under genetic instructions and genetic compulsion, using it to house the species and protect it, assuring permanence.[1]

Thomas doesn't imply that this social behavior is exactly the same for the human species. Indeed he denies it. He says that we are not committed or bound by our genes to stick to one activity forever, like wasps or termits. It is possible for us to change our agendas. We don't have the detailed instructions that other social species have. We can start some things together, drop them, finish them alone, redo them. Nonetheless, while we may not be as specifically programmed as some other species, we are moved toward cooperation, collaboration, and submission (at least partial, if not complete) of the self to the good of the species.

Some research has been done which shows how strong these proclivities toward subordination or cooperation can be. One such study was done by Stanley Milgram at Yale University. Milgram conducted a number of experiments to show the propensity of people to be obedient to authority. He told subjects from the community in New Haven that they were a part of a study on memory and learning. These persons were to teach a "learner" (actually a man who was part of the

19

experimental team) through the use of electric shock. The subjects were told this experiment was a study on the effects of punishment on learning. When the "learner" did not give the correct answer they were to administer what they believed to be an electrical shock (however, the "learner" did not experience the shock, but acted as if he did). At first the subjects thought they were giving a small dose, but when the "learner" performed poorly, the subjects were to increase the punishment to a severe level. When the people increased the shocks to the "learner" this is what happened: "At 120 volts he complains verbally; at 150 he demands to be released from the experiment. His protests continued as the shocks escalated, growing increasingly vehement and emotional. At 285 volts his response can only be described as an agonized scream."[2]

In explaining this behavior on the part of the subjects, Milgram wrote:

> Many subjects will obey the experimenter no matter how vehement the pleading of the person being shocked, no matter how painful the shocks seem to be, and no matter how much the victim pleads to be let out. This was seen time and again in our studies and has been observed in several universities where the experiment was repeated. It is the extreme willingness of adults to go to almost any lengths on the command of an authority that constitutes the chief finding of the study and the fact most urgently demanding explanation. A commonly offered explanation is that those who shocked the victim at the most severe level were monsters, the sadistic fringe of society. But if one considers that almost two-thirds of the participants fall into the category of "obedient" subjects, and that they represented ordinary people drawn from working, managerial, and professional classes, the argument becomes very shaky.[3]

What are Milgram's speculations as to the reasons people obey authority? He gave a number of reasons: some of the subjects thought it would be impolite to challenge the authority; others desired to uphold his or her initial promise of aid to the experimenter; all felt it would have been awkward to withdraw from the experiment.

Some of them became absorbed in the technical aspects of the experiment. Losing sight of the broader (and personal consequences) of behavior, they saw the experiment and themselves as just doing what they were told.

Other subjects, instead of focusing on the moral consequences of their action, focused on the moral consequences of how well they were living up to the expectations of the experimenter.

Many of them harshly devalued the victim in order to justify their action againt him. Once they acted against him, they found it necessary to view him as an unworthy individual whose punishment was made inevitable by his own deficiencies of intellect and character.

Some of the subjects felt it was sufficient for them to recognize that what they were doing was wrong but that it was not necessary for them to act on that belief—that is, make an open break with authority. They derived satisfaction from thinking this was wrong and were on the side of the angels, but they could not muster the inner resources to translate their values into action.

Finally, the subjects showed the tendency we all have toward subordinancy in the presence of authority that was profoundly explored by Sigmund Freud. Freud noticed that many of his patients went through a stage in the therapeutic process where they saw the therapist in the same way that they had seen other important authority figures in their past. He called this "transference," because he believed the patient was transferring the role of the parent, boss, or teacher onto the therapist and responding to the physician in the same manner that he or she responded in the past to these other significant authority persons. In many ways this transference is the same kind of experience that the small child has with its parents. The parents are strong and can protect the child. They are perceived to be very powerful and can get anything for the child that it wants if they choose to provide it.

Transference is not limited to the therapeutic experience. It is a dynamic that is a part of living. People have a tendency to give away some of their autonomy in the hope of getting power to accomplish what they are afraid they cannot do alone. They follow leaders because it is their perception as followers that if they choose to go along with them, some good stuff might rub off on them. They'll get the leader's power, knowledge, skill, mana. To use the language of Erich Fromm:

> In order to overcome his sense of inner emptiness and impotence, [man] . . . chooses an object onto whom he projects all his own human qualities: his love, intelligence, courage, etc. By submitting to this object, he feels in touch with his own qualities; he feels strong, wise, courageous, and secure. To lose the object means the danger of losing himself. This mechanism, idolatric worship of an object, based on the fact of the individual's alienation, is the central dynamism of transference, that which gives transference its strength and intensity.[4]

This is the foundation of dependence and the reason all of us submit to another's leadership. We survive by joining with others to enhance our own power, to strengthen ourselves, to give away some of our own autonomy in hopes of getting power to accomplish something we are afraid we cannot do alone.

This transference was a part of what was happening to me and Tony on the river raft. In my first trip down the river I perceived Tony to be the one with the power and myself to be the "babe." By following Tony, obeying him, seeking his favor, perhaps I could experience the river as a challenge and a thrill instead of a reckless force by which I might be doomed.

The Need to Be Independent

But subordinancy and dependence were not my only experiences with Tony. On the second trip another part of me was emerging. This time Tony was not to be completely in charge of my life. My confidence in confronting the river was increasing, my fear decreasing. On the second trip the river was less of a threat to me, and Tony less of a god. I didn't have to please him in order to survive. The experiences I had had led me to believe I was capable of handling (managing) myself. And, as often happens when a person becomes more confident, in order to prove (test) my power, I challenged the leader whom I believed to be a rival for the control of me. Moreover, as I was developing my own skills in survival, I found it necessary to (I had a need to) express my new confidence. I chose to express that confidence, inappropriately, through challenging and undercutting the leader.

This need to control, to be in charge, to be independent of another's authority or leadership, does not always mean challenging those already in power. Abraham Maslow describes this need for independence as self-actualization and says that people who are self-actualizers (that is, individuals who have matured to a point where they do not need to be dependent on others or to prove their worth by challenging others) have an increased autonomy and resistance to enculturation as well as an increased detachment and desire for privacy. In other words, they can manage very well by themselves. They have little or no need for the approval, support, and attention of others.

It is now in vogue to criticize Maslow's theory because when self-actualization development programs were tried in industry and high premium was placed on worker self-direction and responsibility, some of the workers, who were unwilling to "develop" in this direction, resisted. Other workers who were put with teams of self-actualizers and were expected to function cooperatively had severe difficulties. By their very name, "self-actualizers" are likely to be poor team members and be less interested in getting along with those who need subordinancy.

Others who criticize Maslow are Victor E. Frankl in *Psychotherapy nd Existentialism* (Simon & Shuster, 1968) James MacGregor Burns in *Leadership*, and Daniel Yankelovich in *New Rules* (Random House, 1981). They say that self-actualization is not possible. It is only through interaction with others that one develops, and it is only through interaction with others that one can experience the fulfillment that one seeks. As Burns writes:

> I suggest that the most marked characteristic of self-actualizers as potential leaders goes beyond Maslow's

self-actualization; it is their capacity to *learn* from others and from the environment—the capacity *to be taught*. That capacity calls for an ability to listen and be guided by others without being threatened by them, to be dependent on others but not overly dependent, to judge other persons with both affection and discrimination, to possess enough autonomy to be creative without rejecting the external influences that make for growth and relevance. Self-actualization ultimately means the ability *to lead by being led*.[5]

Burns has gotten to the crux of the matter. It is not that one moves from dependence to autonomy, but rather that one moves within these dichotomous poles: needing both support and control, independence and subordination. Even the wishes of the so-called self-actualizing leader must stay within the bounds of support and common commitment of those who follow. Robert E. Lee was a great general because he was a daring strategist and because he inspired the confidence and support of those who fought under his command. Richard Nixon, on the other hand, was unable to continue as a leader, because he lost the consent of those whose support he needed in order to be effective. Leadership demands the attention of the leader to the needs of the followers. When the leader does not respond to these needs, he or she will soon be alone.

What this means for the management of conflict is that the leader continually faces two questions, Why are these people so passive, not doing anything without my telling them every little thing they must do? and: How can I as leader get these people to stop challenging one another and/or fighting subordinating their individual ideas for the good of the group? The leader can usually respond to

25

one of these two questions and can from time to time encourage autonomy and independence when the individuals are passive, and at the other times discourage self-oriented behavior when it leads to divisiveness among the members or between the members and the leader.

II

The Functions
of Leadership in Conflict:

Arousing Confidence and
Empowering Individuals

In conflict the needs for subordinance (dependence) and autonomy (independence) are experienced more dramatically than in everyday life. Each of these predilections will come to the fore as the conflict increases and will direct the individuals, who are experiencing them, away from the ability to manage the differences. Subordinancy leads the person away from the fray into accommodation and avoidance, and autonomy leads to disengagement, if not attack and attempts to get rid of the other person.

In this chapter and the one immediately following it, I will address these two needs and describe in a general way what a leader needs to do to manage conflict. In the subsequent chapters I will tell how to deal with specific conflict situations.

As we begin, let us define leadership. James MacGregor Burns defines it as follows: "Leadership over human beings is exercised when persons with certain motives and purposes mobilize, in competition or conflict with others, institutional, political, psychological, and other resources so as to arouse, engage, and satisfy the motives of followers."[1] More succinctly, leadership is the mobilization of resources to arouse motives in others. The leader does something that causes another to react favorably. A coach threatens a player with being benched to motivate better play, more effort. A mother praises her child to reinforce and get more positive behavior. The organization's president gives a speech extolling the virtues and values of the new activities that will be possible if the members will vote to raise the dues. These are acts of leadership.

And what are the motives the leader is appealing to? Perhaps, the coach is appealing to the player's pride or desire to be in the game; perhaps, the mother is appealing to the child's needs for approval and support; and perhaps, the president is appealing to the member's needs for community, achievement, and success as an organization. These are some of the myriad motives that empower human behavior.

However, the appeal to motives is only part of Burns' description of leadership. He also differentiates between what he calls transactional and transformational leadership. In *transactional leadership* the leader exchanges goods or services or other things of value, but there is not "a joint effort of persons with common aims acting for the collective interests of all concerned." Burns gives as an example of transactional leadership the colonists in America giving beads to Indians in exchange for Manhattan. Each group got what it wanted, but there was no joint effort for common aims. The Indians wanted beads and the colonists wanted land. *Transformational leadership* on the other hand assumes that the leader and the followers have common goals or interests (though these are not assumed to be 100 percent in agreement), and these goals or interests represent "higher" levels of aspiration than simply meeting the immediate felt needs of the followers. Transformational leadership assumes common purposes or goals and evaluates those goals against standards of improvement rather than simply the satisfaction of needs. Thus, transforming leadership would not stop at focusing on a common interest which is the lowest common denominator (for example, we all want economic stability), but it would also attempt to raise the aspirations of the people to a higher level: we want economic stability in order to provide greater economic justice. So, to use Burns' words, "Transforming leadership ultimately becomes *moral* in that it raises the level of human conduct and ethical aspiration of both leader and led, and thus it has a transforming effect on both."[2]

With these two concerns in mind (leadership has to do with meeting needs and can be either transactional or transformational), the leader needs to perform the following functions to keep the group in conflict healthy:

1. Empower individuals to use their best efforts in the conflict
2. Arouse confidence in the group and its leadership
3. Provide or help the group discover common goals
4. Provide or help the group discover the means of achieving the goals

This chapter will discuss the first two functions and chapter 3 will address the latter two.

As contradictory as it sounds at first, the weaker the people perceive themselves to be, the more likely they will fight dirty or use violence. When one believes he or she is powerless against odds that are too much, he or she is likely to believe that covert action, "dirty" fighting, devious tactics, and violent acts are justified "under the circumstances." Rollo May says that indiviuals or groups use aggression to accomplish a restructuring of power that they cannot achieve by self-affirmation or self-assertion.[3] So, in a sense, it can be said that violence is a function of powerlessness; the more powerless a person feels the more likely he or she is to attack or to attempt to get rid of or punish the other person.

As a leader in conflict empowering the other means helping the other person feel strong enough to use his or her best self and best means to accomplish whatever ends are deemed important. In fact, the leader's self-protective instincts tend to move in the opposite direction. Instead of strengthening those who are in conflict with the leader or the group, the tendency is to weaken them—make them feel powerless to do more harm, demean them, devastate them, put them down—for by so doing the leader will feel stronger, more powerful, more able to care for himself or herself.

Transactional Leadership

Empowering others means that *transformational leadership* is used to help them feel strong enough to deal with the issues and the relationships that are confronting the organization. *Transactional leadership* leaves everybody where they were when the conflict began. In transactional leadership dependent persons are taken care of, things are done for them, and they are given what they want. When the leader does for the dependent persons, she or he is keeping them subordinate. The leader has the power and takes the risk and the blame; the follower has the safety and the protection and accuses, is negative, complains, and cries. In transactional leadership the leader (who we assume is not dependent) has power and protects the follower, making him feel safe. For this the leader receives obedience, and servitude. And if these followers' needs are not met, their demands increase and they blame or punish the leader. Sometimes the leader is destroyed, fired, or punished for not meeting the needs

30

of the dependents. Unless the dependent is somehow empowered to move out of this state, she or he will not become an independent or interdependent person. Transactional leadership leaves the leader powerless to do anything except respond to the needs of those who cannot take care of themselves.

For example, I have a client with whom I have been working for about two years. When I started working with this man, he had a conflict with another man on his staff. Because of the level of fear that was present in these two people and their long history of dirty fighting, when there was a problem neither would go to the other to work it out. They would call me and complain. I would respond to the complaints by bearing each antagonist's message to the other and then I would set up a meeting where I told each of them what they had to do and how to do it. This worked surprisingly well on two occasions. On the third occasion when I was called, I realized that I had been doing for them rather than helping them develop capabilities to enable them to work through their own difficulties. Abruptly I suggested to each one that he go to the other and try to work things out. Without preparation, skill, or the support they had come to expect, they quickly made a full-scale war out of a question of protocol.

Transactional leadership can be as useless as well for those with high needs for independence. If what the person needs is a chance to do things alone, to prove that he or she is competent, or better than others, the transactional leader is likely to try to meet this need in order to get the other to do what the leader wants. For example, the leader wants a particular individual to chair the fund-raising committee. The woman accepts the job as chairperson on the condition that she can do things her way, and the job is set up in such a way that her needs for independence are met. The more her needs are met the further she gets from the organization's purposes and plans. And if she is challenged, what is she likely to do—the only thing a person with needs to be independent can do, quit or attack the person who has invaded her "turf."

In other words just meeting the needs with which you are presented is likely to lead you into further difficulty in the long run, especially in conflict.

Transformational Leadership

A transformational leader is influential in strengthening and inspiring the follower rather than trading with or overpowering him or her. The leader arouses confidence in the follower that she is able to accomplish whatever goals they share. McClelland wrote in *Power: The Inner Experience*[4] that the leader's message is not so much, "Do as I say because I am strong and know best. You are children with no wills of your own and must follow me because I know better," but rather "Here are the goals which are true and right and which we share. Here is how we can reach them. You are strong and capable. You can accomplish these goals." In an article in *Daedalus*, Richard Tucker described a transformational leader as one who typically radiates a buoyant confidence in the rightness and goodness of the aims that he proclaims for the movement, in the practical possibility of attaining these aims, and in his own special calling and capacity to provide the requisite leadership. Needless to say, in the lives of most of these leaders—even those who do achieve success—there are moments of discouragement and despair when they and their cause seem fated to fail.

32

But it is not characteristic of them to display such feelings in public. Rather, they show a stubborn self-confidence and faith in the movement's prospects of victory and success.[5]

So, one of the functions of the transformational leader is to empower by arousing confidence—confidence in the cause and confidence in the leader. But there is more to transformational leadership than engendering resolution and equanimity. The transformational leader recognizes the arrays of motives and goals of the followers, helps bring them to consciousness, helps people meet their needs, and helps them redefine their aspirations to higher levels.

These aspirations can be at many levels and have many dimensions ranging from values about food to values about liberty, national identity, or justice. Let us take only the needs for autonomy and subordinancy and review the transformational leader's function in relation to them.

In order to do this we will look at the developmental stages of power for an individual as developed by McClelland. He says that the first stage of power development is weakness, a feeling that one has no power of her own. She needs the leader to provide it. It is like being a baby who needs mommy or daddy to give her something to eat. The baby feels strong when it is fed. It feels good when it has been strengthened by others. This, of course, is the need we call dependence.

The second stage of power development is the individual beginning to control herself. The baby begins to walk, to talk, to move hands and legs in ways that accomplish feats of skill; the baby learns that she is in charge of her own body and begins to use the word "no."

In the third stage the person tests her skills against other's skills and thinks, How do I know I am a good

33

artist? My painting is better than yours. How do I know I am strong? I can get you to do what I want you to do. This is the adolescent stage of the developing person, the stage that is often called counter-dependent because the growing person tests maturity by challenging or going against the leader, the authority, the one on whom he or she has been dependent. This stage is critical for the development of groups, because the followers need a chance to test their skills against the person or persons who have up to this time been their providers of power (or safety) or they will likely get stuck in stage two. It is fitting for one to try his or her strength against those who have been trusted. This testing will help the individual see if the leader (as the parent or authority figure) is strong enough to accept challenges. How devastating it would be if the leader caved in, if the leader is overpowered, if the leader gave up when challenged.

Here challenge tests the authority's authenticity. Are you real? Have you really been giving me good stuff? Will your stuff work against strong challenges? Is your stuff worth modeling?

In the fourth stage I move beyond my concern for myself and concern for you. I begin to see that I do not have enough power alone and you do not have enough power alone to accomplish something important beyond our individual selves. In this stage I see that our joining together can accomplish more for the good of all than my focusing solely on myself and my own individual needs or on you and your competencies and incompetencies.

The task of the transformational leader in all of this is to recognize where people are in their maturation and work with them as they go through each stage. This is complicated, obviously. Some with whom you are working are in the first stages of subordinancy; others are in the fourth stage of interdependence. It is the task of the leader to work with people as they move up and through the stage they are currently in. The leader needs to help the person in stage one carry out tasks alone. Here the key issues will be first to help people see where they are now and then to assist through encouragement and training, to start being independent by doing tasks that are manageable and have a high probability of success so that they do not become discouraged. Give feedback, both negative and positive when appropriate. Telling them how they are doing is not only important for your relationship, but it also lets them know that you think their job is important to you and to the organization. (In other words, you are using the subordinancy need to help the person develop independence.)

For the person who is doing very well alone, who doesn't need or want to be with the rest of the group, who is busy showing off how well she is progressing, the next stage is to test her new-found skills against what she has previously done. The stage-two person should be encouraged to challenge the system, to think of new aproaches, to engage in limited conflict with others in the organization. The learning here is that conflict can be managed; it will not destroy the person. It is something that can be dealt with, both by the leader and by the follower. Without moving into this stage of testing, we do not learn how to appreciate the fact that others have good ideas too, that our ideas are not always appreciated by others, and that by surfacing the issues and dealing with them we are more likely to find mutually satisfactory solutions than if we force our own way on others, or accommodate to another's way or wishes.

In this third stage the task is to affirm the possibilities of conflict in the relationship and attempt to move from distributive to integrative problem-solving techniques. Distributive techniques assume that the best solution of the problem is my solution. Distributive techniques assume that when there is a problem, it is not so much a problem to be solved but a contest that will have a winner and a loser. Now, in the midst of the conflict, we can see the integrative possibilities, that you can have some of what you want and I can have some of what I want, and we do not have to end up with victors and losers.

In each of these stages of development fear is generated by each transition and especially by the conflict in moving through and out of stage three.

Thus, the transformational leader will join those with whom she is working, not just to meet the needs presented by the stage in which they are presently existing, but also to help them experience and explore the possibilities of growth.

Before moving on to the later two functions of leadership in conflict, I would like to remind you that arousing confidence in followers does not necessarily mean that the leader is likable or will have close, friendly relations with others. In an experiment with executives, McClelland and Burnham found that those who had high needs for power were much more likely to lead successful departments than those who had high needs for affiliation.

> We worked first with sales departments, dividing them evenly between those with above average and those with below average sales. Only 20 percent of the better half were run by managers with a higher need for affiliation than for power. But 90 percent of the poorer ones were run by affiliatives. So power managers ran 80 percent of the best, only 10 percent of the worst. . . . In other departments (design, development, production) we

found the same line between the manager's drive and the department's performance. Affiliative managers ran only 27 percent of the better departments, but 78 percent of the weaker half. On the other hand, power managers ran 73 percent of the good ones, only 22 percent of the weak ones.

McClelland believes that affiliative types get into trouble as leaders because they want to be liked. This leads them to make wishy-washy decisions. They want to be on good terms with everyone, and they care more about the well-being of individuals than the group as a whole. This puts them in positions where they are likely to make exceptions to organization policy, thus violating one of bureaucracy's first principles—fairness. Helping one at the expense of the group can alienate many. The failure to treat people equally undermines other people's faith in the corporate reward system, so that inconsistent decisions may make the subordinates feel powerless to control events by their behavior.

III

The Functions
of Leadership:

Finding Goals and a Means of Achieving Them

Developing Group Goals

The third function of leadership is purposefully given an ambiguous title because it refers either to giving the group a vision or helping the group discover its vision. Much of the literature on management is about helping the group do its own research to discover the needs of the individuals who are a part of the group, the needs in the environment which they are seeking to address, and the needs of the group itself.

Current management theory strongly emphasizes the importance of each individual member's motivation, in addition to the needs for dependence and independence. People act, participate, work in groups that are helping them meet their own personal needs. For example, David Berlew, in his article "Leadership and Organizational Excitement," says that individuals participate in organizations in hopes of finding (in order to meet personal needs) sources of meaning or excitement which may be lacking in other parts of their lives. Berlew believes that the major "opportunities" (that is, motivators) are these:

Sources of Meaning in Organizations: Opportunities and Related Values

Type of Opportunity	Related Need or Value
1. A chance to be tested; to make it on one's own	Self-reliance Self-actualization
2. A social experiment, to combine work, family, and play in some new way	Community Integration of life
3. A chance to do something well—for instance, return to real craftsmanship; to be really creative	Excellence Unique accomplishment
4. A chance to do something good—for instance, run an honest, no "rip-off," business or a youth counseling center	Consideration Service
5. A chance to change the way things are—for instance, from Republican to Democrat or Socialist, from war to peace, from unjust to just	Activism Social responsibility Citizenship

But these individual needs are not the only goal factors that shape organizational life. While every individual brings his or her own needs (goals) to the organization, the organization also has purposes that are common to the members. It is good when the common goal or goals meet the individual needs of some or of all the members. However, in some instances of organizational life the common task is not relevant to the needs of the members, but it affords opportunities for other needs to be met. For example, getting out mailings for a political candidate is likely not meeting the volunteer's need for self-reliance, excellence, or consideration. However, the relationships that are developed in the work, the importance of the end product, and the feeling of being "in" the campaign may well be fulfilling.

In order to find and agree on the common goal factors the members of the organization must agree on what its common purposes are. If these common purposes relate to the environment outside the boundaries of the membership, then some kind of assessment will have to be made to discover how to relate to that environment. To illustrate, if the organization is trying to elect a candidate to office, the campaign committee should do something about the needs and wants of the others who will actually do the electing; if it is trying to sell a product, it will have to know about the needs and wants of the buyers; if it is attempting to provide a service to others, it will have to know what kinds of services are needed and wanted by those outside the organization.

The needs of the group itself must also be assessed. By group needs I am talking about those factors that are necessary for the group to maintain itself. If it has a paid staff, it will need money for salaries. The group needs a system for communicating among the members, processes for managing conflict and differences when they arise, processes to support members in their work and a system for evaluating their progress, and other maintenance factors too numerous to list here.

The usual processes for helping a group of people discover what their needs are, the needs of those in the environment they are trying to serve, and the needs of the group itself can be found in many resources.[1] All these resources agree that the leadership of the organization must provide a means by which the needs of the individuals, environment, and group are discovered or clarified and must make decisions as to which needs will be addressed first and how they will be met (who will do what). The methods of gathering information can vary from questionnaires, to observation, to small group discussion, to interviews, to analyzing demographic studies. It is not the purpose of this book to explain these processes in detail. If you are interested in this material, may I suggest that you go to the sources listed.

Methods of self-assessment by members of the group are excellent and useful, but they are not the only way groups clarify their purposes. Leaders themselves can give the group its common vision and goals. This is risky. Some leaders don't have good or exciting ideas. Some don't know how to articulate the ideas they have in a way that captures the imagination and enthusiasm of others, and that is only half of it. As a group matures, as we saw in earlier chapters, the members may resist dependence on the leader for guidance, direction, enlivenment. In fact, at some stages of the group life, the leader's support for any idea may generate substantial resistance on the part of some members who need to prove themselves by challenging the leader.

Nonetheless, the importance of the leader in helping the group find or see its mission is critical. A recent analysis of leadership in the army makes these points vividly. Gabriel and Savage, in their book *Crisis in Command*,[2] asked the question, Why was there such poor morale and low effectiveness in the Vietnam experience? They concluded that there were two major reasons: "careerism," and the assumption by high-level staff

41

officers at the Pentagon that men could be "managed" to their death. The careerism issue has to do with the fact that the army had begun to develop and adopt a new ethical code rooted in what Gabriel and Savage called the entrepreneurial model of the modern business corporation. In business it is expected that the leader will operate out of a code of ethics drawn largely from the practices of the free-enterprise marketplace. With regard to one's career, most of the institutional reinforcement for officer behavior tends to support careerism, self-seeking, the use of one's charge and command largely as a means to higher career rewards. The advancement of one's career was the primary value in the army in Vietnam rather than focusing on the traditional, higher values of duty, honor, and country.

The other part of Gabriel and Savage's critique of the U.S. Vietnam military experience had to do with the command's placing primary importance on management rather than commitment. Officers were rotated so often (based on rational decisions for advancement, variety of experience, and the needs for R and R) that they lost their ability to identify with their units and become a part of a team which was engaged in an important struggle together. These rational policies and the ethics of efficiency that supported them meant that the officer was less concerned about troop welfare and less willing to share the risks of battle. Gabriel and Savage say, in contrast to army policy, that the marks of a good officer are: "They were available to their men; they accepted an inordinate share of the burden of death; they were professionally competent and reliable, and, very importantly, they were present at the front." These are the things that kept the combat groups together as primary units. When rotation is necessary, what can be done (as the Germans did in World War II) is to rotate divisions out of the line for reconstitution of their primary groups rather than rotating individuals in and out of the groups, especially the officers. What happened in Vietnam was that the U.S. gave up a sense of belonging for a sense of cost effectiveness. Expanding on this point, they wrote:

> General Maxwell Taylor once suggested that the Army "is more like a church." While the suggestion may be too strong insofar as organized religious creeds often call for the abandonment of the self and, at times, even the family in total devotion to one's beliefs, it is not incorrect to suggest that the analogy of the military life to that of a monastery may be more accurate. What religious orders and successful military organizations—by which we mean those that can establish functional combat units which cohere under combat stress—have in common in that both have established what might be called the "price of belonging" and have evolved a set of behavioral guidelines for demonstrating how that "price" is to be paid. To speak of the "price of belonging" is to suggest that there is a common code of ethics agreed on and observed to such an extent that one's definition of what one truly is, is defined in terms of one's ability and willingness to observe the code. Accordingly, a monk is said to be a good monk when he observes and practices the values which the monastic order holds dear. Analogously, a "good" officer is one who recognizes a set of values and obligations which are common to his brother officers and observes them, demanding a high degree of selflessness. Entrance into the community is predicated upon recognition and observance of commonly held values. One is sustained within the community by strict fidelity to such values.[3]

The point of this discussion of the army and its leaders is: in order for the leader to be effective, he or she must not only articulate the values of the group, but also live them, taking the same risks and getting involved at the same level in the same work. Thus, from within the life of the group—by participating in it—the officer may then provide the leadership that will be listened to, understood, appreciated, incorporated by those who follow.

From this base, then, the leader can use techniques which express what he or she hopes might become the common vision of the group with which he is working, such as,

> appealing to the emotions and values of others
> activating members' personal commitment to private hopes and ideals
> sharing ideas about the exciting possibilities that lie ahead
> identifying common strengths the members of the group have
> articulating shared dreams, values, common interests
> using word pictures and imagery to describe the future
> communicating through a style that is congruent with the excitement of the message: gestures, eye contact, facial expression, voice intensity, energy, etc.
> emphasizing what *we* can accomplish together, if *we* all join together.[4]

Helping the Group Find Means of Achieving Its Goals

Nothing will immobilize a group faster than having exciting goals and believing that it is impossible to reach them. Martin Seligman says that the most critical self-appraisal a human being can make has to do with being in control. If a person learns that her responses make no difference toward obtaining predictable outcomes, she experiences a loss of control. "Motivation to

44

behave drops dramatically, and severe depression is the emotional outcome." Seligman's research indicates that one of the causes of depression is the belief that action is futile. The depression-prone individual is one who reacts to a variety of life events by generating a series of thoughts that accumulate to form the appraisal: "My behavior really makes no difference in these situations. I am not in control of my environment." He says that:

> The depressed patient believes or has learned that he cannot control those elements of his life that relieve suffering, bring gratification, or provide nurture—in short, he believes that he is helpless. Consider a few of the precipitating events: What is the meaning of job failure or incompetence at school? Often it means that all of a person's efforts have been in vain, that his responses have failed to achieve his desires. When an individual is rejected by someone he loves, he can no longer control this significant source of gratification and support. When a parent or lover dies, the bereaved is powerless to elicit love from the dead person. Physical disease and growing old are helpless conditions par excellence; the person finds his own responses ineffective and is thrown upon the care of others.[5]

A group of people can become just as depressed as individuals. It is the task of the leader to help people see and believe that they have ways to achieve their goals. There are four things that leaders often do to help alleviate these feelings of powerlessness: create success experiences, help only when asked, encourage collaboration, and reward rather than punish group members.

Creating success experiences means that the leader helps the group have a positive experience and a sense of movement in its work. If I am successful at level one, perhaps I can be successful at the next level as well. One of our children had difficulty learning to drive with a stick shift car; after numerous failures at getting the car to move smoothly or to keep the engine running, he just about gave up hope of learning to drive. He then tried a car with an automatic shift. After learning to drive this car, he had enough confidence to tackle the other more difficult vehicle.

Berlew says it is extremely difficult to help someone without making him feel weaker, since the act of helping makes evident the fact that you are more knowlegeable, more powerful, wiser, or richer than the person you are trying to help.[6] Perhaps the most notable large-scale example of this is the "thanks" the United States has gotten from underdeveloped nations during and after our aid programs. When our help is given in such a way as to emphasize the "one-down" position of the other, it clearly continues to alienate, rather than ingratiate us to them. Berlew writes:

> The effective . . . leader gives his subordinates as much control over the type and amount of help they want as he can without taking untenable risks. He makes his help readily available to those who might come looking for it, and he gives it in such a way as to minimize their dependence upon him. Perhaps most importantly, he is sensitive to situations where he himself can use help and he asks for it, knowing that giving help will strengthen the other person and make him better able to receive help.

Encouraging collaboration is also a critical leadership skill at this stage. To collaborate means to co-labor, to work together. Here we are very concerned with the subordinancy issues we have spoken of before. By "doing-for" one sabotages helping the other develop into stages two, three, and four. But not only is "doing-for" a

46

problem, so is abdicating, standing off rather than seeing if the assigned task is done correctly. An effective leader joins with her followers in the accomplishment of their common goals.

Finally, reward rather than punishment is critical for the development of strength within the group. From the research of behavioral scientists in operant conditioning we know that non-reward extinguishes a behavior that is not wanted or is inappropriate. Glenna Joyce Holsinger wrote in *The Personnel Administrator:*

> We have stopped excessive gossiping or talking and excessive complaining or griping by using strategies depending mainly on the principle of extinction. In one company, a key manager in the manufacturing division spent an average of two hours a day discussing the weather, politics, scouting, and management theory with any employee he could corner. By teaching key people how to respond to him, the time spent gossiping and talking fell to 10 minutes a day within a month. The main point to remember is that by ignoring the most negative behavior and reinforcing an opposite (incompatible) positive response, attitudes and behavior change rapidly.[7]

But rewarding positive behavior or punishing negative behavior can exhaust tremendous amounts of time. We know that punishment only works as a temporary solution to suppress or weaken a behavior. Reward is also short-lived unless it is kept up. Therefore, the trick for the leader is to help the follower find rewards which are intrinsic to the behavior he wants to support rather than finding it necessary to spend his time running around praising people for a good job (or punishing them for not doing well).

Some jobs have built-in punishment for doing well. I

know of a church that rewards persons who do a good job on one committee by asking them to serve on two or more committees the next year. Those who are smart in that church know to lie low for fear of being overwhelmed with requests for work from well-meaning people who end up punishing those who do their jobs well.

Further, rewarding the worker does not and should not mean that the leader ends up praising everybody all the time (although a little praise is certainly appreciated). The issue is not to praise or punish but to find ways that workers can find meaning and reward in the work that they do. Often this is done through evaluation (note the roots of the word "e-valuation" which means getting value out of) which can be done by helping the worker discover what she is getting from the job. This means avoiding overpraising (which is perceived as gratuitous) or doing the work for her (which creates more dependence). Evaluation helps the worker find value in doing what all agree is important.

These two concerns, helping the group define its common goals and finding ways of achieving them, are absolutely critical in conflict management. Until the members can see purposes that divide them, the conflict will remain and may escalate out of control. These two themes tie in with transforming leadership and empowerment, as well. Transforming leadership helps the group look beyond that which divides to see the common purposes and hopes that may provide the glue of unity. Further, the very essence of empowerment is helping people find a way (a means) to do that which they have felt helpless to accomplish by themselves.

IV

Fear and Conflict

Just as profound as the internal drives toward independence and cooperation is the function of fear in a conflict situation. Fear is what you experience emotionally when you perceive that you are being threatened by danger or evil and you feel incompetent to manage it. Actually fear is only a part of the total human response to a threat. The term that is usually used to describe this general response is "stress." Hans Selye, a professor at the University of Montreal, gave this word its medical usage. In his research of the bodily reactions to just about every conceivable type of crisis—severe injury, disease, poison, excessive stimulation, or unusual work demand—Selye found that there were certain features common to all of them. In addition to specific changes—the rash of measles, the local bruise of an injury—some "nonspecific" reactions were found. He called these nonspecific reactions "stress."

The initial part of stress is what he called the "alarm" reaction. In this stage messages from the brain, acting through the hypothalamus, stimulate the sympathetic nerves and the pituitary which trigger an outpouring of adrenaline from the adrenal glands. This reaction stimulates the heart and blood pressure, the muscles and the lungs, and improves blood flow, oxygen consumption, and strength. Simultaneously it activates the liver, spleen, and other necessary organs, and deactivates some others such as the digestive system. These reactions are "nonspecific," because they do not occur in just one or two stressful situations. They are a part of what he called the "General Adaptation Syndrome," or what others have called the "General Stress Syndrome." Selye called this syndrome "adaptive" because it is essential to human survival. Without it we may not be prepared to respond to real threats.

These responses to stress are not always adaptive, however; in his book, *Stress Without Distress*, Selye points out that inflammation is a basic physiological defense mechanism. Its main purpose is to localize irritants by putting a barricade of inflammatory tissue around them. This process prevents blood poisoning by inhibiting the spread of microbes into the blood. This adaptive response in one situation (in response to a cut) can be maladaptive in another.

> Here, inflammation itself is what we experience as a disease. Thus in many patients who suffer from hay fever or extreme swelling after an insect sting, suppression of defensive inflammation is essentially the cure. This is because the invading stressor agent is not in itself dangerous or likely to spread and kill. In the case of grafts, it may even be lifesaving.[1]

Stress has not only physiological components, but emotional components as well. "Emotion" has as its root the Latin word *movere* which is the verb "to move." *Movere*, combined with other English words, means to move strongly (commotion), to move away from (demotion), to move forward (promotion), to move back (remove). "E-motion" is to move out from. Fear is the emotion that moves one strongly out from threat. The "e" prefix implies that one gets motion out of or adds motion to. For example, in the word "e-valuate," the "e" prefix implies that one gets the value out of something or adds value to it, not "de-value" which is taking value from. An emotion, then, adds impetus. The emotion fear provides the impetus to act. The emotion drives or helps push people to respond to the difficulties they are facing.

We tend to quickly assess our environment as threatening and dangerous. John Parrino writes in his book, *From Panic to Power*:

> Some investigators feel that humans are biologically programmed to respond to the dangerous element in the environment because of the efficacy of this response in facilitating survival. Early humans had to size up their environments quite rapidly in order to appraise the danger that was constantly lurking there. This ability to size up dangerous and threatening situations paid off in terms of survival. In the same manner, thinking patterns that were slow and insensitive to threats were readily extinguished.
>
> Other investigators emphasize the importance of early social learning in programming humans to respond in a highly threatened fashion to life events. Adults are constantly coping in a high-pressured and irrational world and easily transmit their thoughts and internalized strategies to the younger, more vulnerable members of society. Perhaps the most adequate explanation that accounts for the human tendency to be easily threatened by the environment is a biosocial one, that is, biological tendencies and social learning contribute equally to our tendency to appraise life events as threatening and dangerous.

Thus, our quick response to fear is what we have been taught by our parents and what we are programmed, genetically, to do. To add insult to injury, this initial assessment may well influence a person's subsequent thoughts and images so that self-dialogue becomes programming for danger. Each subsequent thought or external event aggravates an already alerted and frightened response system. This "alerted" or frightened reasoning system becomes one of the major problems in managing conflict.

Therefore, let us look in more detail at the reasoning process of a person in conflict. Aaron Beck has studied the role of faulty thinking patterns and their relationship to negative emotional states. He says that persons under stress tend to engage regularly in the following thought patterns:

> *Dichotomous reasoning:* to think in terms of extremes or opposites. Internalized statements that indicate a tendency to think in absolutes are: "Everyone is against me." "Nobody seems to like me."
>
> *Overgeneralization:* to generate a series of thoughts and beliefs on the basis of a small amount of data. An individual who overgeneralizes allows one incident of failure and criticism to influence thoughts and attitudes about other similar incidences. "I'll never confide in my boss again. He'll always criticize me and see me as a failure."
>
> *Magnification:* to view events as much more threatening and dangerous than they really are. Hypochondriacs, for example, assume that each ache and pain in their body represents the beginning of a dreaded disease.
>
> *Arbitrary inference:* to base beliefs and conclusions on evidence that is totally unrelated to the context of the present situation. This tendency reflects a failure in discrimination. For example, the boss' bad mood is taken very personally. "I don't know why he or she is mad at me. I didn't do anything to warrant that reaction."

Usually in dichotomous reasoning a person sees problems as stemming from either his or her inadequacy or another person's inadequacy. And often one individual will choose one assessment consistently over the other. To quote from Richard Lazarus:

> Consider two different persons who perceive that they are facing a demand, or the juxtaposition of several demands, which seems to them to be at the borderline or beyond their capacity to master—too much is expected of them. As a result of their individual histories and particular personalities, Person A feels that failure of mastery reflects his own inadequacy, while Person B, by contrast, feels the same inadequacy but interprets the situation as one in which people are constantly trying to use or abuse him. Both experience similar degrees of anticipatory stress and are mobilized to cope with the problem. Prior to the confrontation that will reveal the success or failure of mastery, both experience anxiety, and anticipatory emotion in the context of appraised threat. In Person A, the anxiety is mixed, perhaps with anticipatory depression, while in Person B, the anxiety is mixed with external blaming and anger. Following confrontation in which, let us say, both perform badly, Person A experiences mainly loss and depression, while Person B experiences mainly anger and resentment. A similar set of overwhelming demands have been construed or appraised quite differently because of different personality dispositions. If these persons do well in the confrontation, both may experience elation because they have overcome the difficulty, depending on whether the explanation of the success is luck or their own perseverance and skill.[2]

These distortions in thinking are not uncommon in situations of stress. Usually, however, in the first stages of experiencing threat the arousal of fear is not great enough to disable thinking or to lead to distorted thinking processes. Often a motivator (e-motion) can cause a person to know a problem exists and that action should be taken to deal with it. *The learning for the leader,* here, is to know that it is wiser to take action quickly rather than to wait until the levels of emotion become high and the stress or fear seriously interferes with rational thinking processes. As the fear increases so does the tendency toward distorted thinking which will probably be the most severe problem that you as a leader will have to deal with when confronted by conflict in your organization.

The leader can use two approaches to deal with distorted thinking. The first is desensitization to the threatening stimuli and the second is challenging the problematic thinking style.

Desensitization

Desensitization is repeated exposure to events that are threatening to the individual. Dr. Joseph Wolpe's work with phobiacs showed that as a result of repeated exposure fearful individuals reduced their anxiety in situations which aroused their fears. Parrino, in *From Panic to Power*, describes Wolpe's method as follows:

> In desensitization the phobic individual imagines a gradual confrontation with the feared situation while in a deep state of relaxation. The desensitization trainer closely monitors the phobic's emotional reactions and never allows the individual to experience high levels of anxiety while he or she is imagining the scene. The fearful stimulus is presented in stages. For example, a person who is afraid of heights may first imagine climbing one step of a ten-step ladder. Each stage is taken gradually, and the least threatening step in chain of responses [sic] toward the feared object is accomplished before the next step is taken. When all of the steps are completed in imagery, the individual is then ready to confront the fearful situation in reality. According to Wolpe, the most important component of this fear reduction process is the

association between low levels of bodily arousal and the feared stimulus. As long as a state of relaxation is present during each exposure the stimulus cannot elicit the fear response.

This information can be highly useful to you as a leader in a conflict situation. Assume that two persons are in conflict. What often happens is that each avoids the other and opportunity for desensitization does not occur. Or, the two parties try to have a "confrontation," and what occurs is not a gradual stage-by-stage movement toward the arena that is causing the difficulty, but a sudden leap at the problem, a surge of fear and anger, followed by withdrawal. Both parties leave the situation again confirmed in their perception that this is "too hot to handle."

If you have a conflict with another person, I recommend that you move toward the other in small steps. It is better to start moving toward the other in fantasy as Wolpe recommends, and then gradually attempt stage-by-stage to connect with the other person, at first on superficial levels and then on the level of the conflict. This stage-by-stage system starts with the recognition that repeated attempts will be necessary (not just one great denouement as occurs in the movies). Recognizing in the beginning that this won't be easy will help greatly to deal with the problem.

When the problem is not between you and another but between others within the organization, take each person through one, two, three, or four dry runs before helping them actually "confront" one another. Then as you take them into the encounter do it slowly, by degrees, in many cases trying not to solve the whole thing in one meeting, but taking it a piece at a time.

55

Challenging Problematic Thinking

The other approach to help manage the disordered thinking component in a conflict situation is challenging and changing problem-thinking styles. This is most easily done when you recognize that your thinking is disordered. I can recognize when my thinking is likely to be disordered by these signs:

I have thoughts of losing control

I am afraid that I will get hurt or the other will get hurt

I am afraid that I or the other person will not be able to handle the situation

I find it very difficult to concentrate. (Irving Janis called this hypervigilance where one makes a snap judgment and comes up with simple-minded answers. Often the person starts dividing everything into dichotomous or black and white/good and evil categories at this stage.)

If these warning signs are not clue enough, review Albert Ellis' following list of the ten most common irrational ideas and see if they fit the kind of thoughts you are having in the conflict situation.

Ten Most Common Irrational Ideas

1. It is a dire necessity for an adult to be loved or approved by almost everyone for virtually every-thing he does.
2. One should be thoroughly competent, adequate, and achieving in all possible respects.
3. Certain people are bad, wicked or villainous and they should be severely blamed and punished for their sins.
4. It is terrible, horrible, and catastrophic when things are not going the way one would like them to go.

5. Human unhappiness is externally caused and people have little or no ability to control their sorrows or rid themselves of their negative feelings.

6. If something is or may be dangerous or fearsome, one should be terribly occupied with and upset about it.

7. It is easier to avoid facing many life difficulties and self-responsibilities than to undertake more rewarding forms of self-discipline.

8. The past is all-important and because something once strongly affected one's life, it should indefinitely do so.

9. People and things should be different from the way they are, and it is catastrophic if perfect solutions to the grim realities of life are not immediately found.

10. Maximum human happiness can be achieved by inertia and inaction or by passively and uncommittedly enjoying oneself.

Of course, it is easier to deal with disordered thinking if you recognize that you are experiencing it. Further, it is easier to deal with it in a non-threatening situation than in a threatening situation. Another way to evaluate your thinking is to use the questions developed by Colleen Kelly in *Assertion Training*[3] for reflecting on your own and others' thinking:

Is this a realistic belief? What evidence do I have that this may or may not happen or be true?

Even if this is a realistic belief, is it as terrible an occurrence as I am imagining? How would I handle this if it happened?

Is holding this belief helping me to act the way I want to act in this situation?

How would I feel if I were the other person? What do other people think would be the logical consequence of being assertive in this situation?

What challenges might I use to counter this fear?

A challenge is a thought to put in the place of the disordered or irrational thought. For example, I may have the disabling image: I have to please everbody all the time. It can be replaced with: it would be nice if everyone liked me, but I know that some will not and most will like me most of the time, but not all the time.

Helping Others Deal with Their Problematic Thinking

Up to this point I have been describing what you can do to deal with your own disordered thinking. What can be done when you see this kind of thinking in a person with whom you are having conflict? First, let me say that *it is not a good idea to suggest to the other that his or her idea is irrational* and that it must be replaced with more rational thoughts. The use of such an abrupt assessment will only harden the other person's recalcitrance. It is better to *point out those beliefs that you do not perceive to be realistic and to suggest a substitute for the disabling image.* For example, if a person suggests that your reason for not appointing her to the nominating committee was motivated by your discomfort with females, you might suggest that you are comfortable with females and *then give the real reason* you left her off the committee. Sometimes you will find that giving the real reason is not adequate, the other will continue to hold the original negative idea, but if you can state it more than once and bolster it with evidence to support your position you will be in better shape than just saying it once and letting it go at that.

When the conflict is between others, and you are not one of the antagonists (or perhaps I should say protagonists), your job will not be as awkward. If you have the trust of all parties, go to each one and help him or her identify the irrational ideas that might be getting in the way. For example, I was working with the white director of a volunteer agency in Detroit who believed that certain people on his staff would not cooperate with him and his programs simply because he was not black. I did not impudently say that this was certainly irrational thinking and that he ought to replace it with more productive thoughts. Instead, I gently asked, "Alan, what evidence do you have that this belief may or may not be true?" Each of the instances that he related were assessments that he had made based on speculations in his own head, or what I usually call "attributions"; they were not statements based on the real, direct experience of the director. I pointed this out to him. I then asked how he could get evidence to prove or disprove these attributions. We identified a couple of people whose opinion he trusted and from whom he thought he could get a straight story. He then went to them and asked their opinions and found his attributions to be inappropriate. This was not to say that everything he turned up was positive. He did find a good deal of negative feeling about his leadership, but the reason for it was not his race. It was for some specific actions that he had taken toward other employees the year before.

In some cases it will not be possible for the leader to get the confirming (or disconfirming) data. When this happens, and this should be a second choice, let someone else ask others what their opinions and feelings are. The third party can then take this information back to the leader who may be making the attributions. If you are the third party, it is important that the one with the attributions wants the information and thinks it's a good idea for you to get it. Further, it is helpful if he or she helps you think about how you will get the data so that there will be a higher probability of "ownership" of the data when it is collected.

In dealing with the effects of fear on conflict management, you will not only want to be aware of the effect of the fears on the rational thinking processes, but you will also want to take into account the causes of the fears in the first place. Many times the leader can directly allay the fears of the person with whom he or she is in conflict. If you can identify the sources of these fears, it will give you the option of responding so as to allay the fear, if you choose to. Common fears in conflict are:

I might lose my job, position, or standing in the group
I might make a mistake
The other might not like what I am doing
The other might not like me
I might be criticized
I might impose
The other might leave

Behind these fears may be the fear of rejection, fear of failure, and sometimes the fear of success. Fear of rejection is most common and certainly related to the concern we talked about in the first chapter about dependency or the need we all have to be related to other people. This strong need is often at the root of the fear of being left alone—you might not want to be with me if you find out what I'm really like. Certainly, those unpleasant experiences of childhood rejection are remembered and reexperienced when the threat of another rejection (probable or improbable) is encountered. Those early memories again become present in the now and are experienced along with the already painful present.

Fear of failure is another profound fear that inhibits our ability to stay in conflict in a healthy way. Failure can be translated as death or losing control. Fear of failure is my fear that I might mess up so badly that I will be destroyed—my career wrecked—I will be unable to cope—I will ruin the organization that I admire and hope will continue to be effective. Where fear of rejection is related to our need for relationship, fear of failure is related to survival. I must take care of myself first and then be concerned about others.

A special case of fear of failure is fear of success or what Freud called the "wrecked by success syndrome." Here the fear is that if I keep doing well and improving, I will reach a level where I will be unable to continue and my whole world will fall apart. This is the fear on which Laurence J. Peter capitalized with his "Peter Principle," that "in a hierarchy every employee tends to rise to the level of his incompetence." This is the fear that I have been successful up to now, but soon time will come when I will be unable to cope and my incompetence will show to the whole world.

One of the main tasks of the leader, then, will be to help people allay these fears, especially in conflict, in which they tend to be exacerbated. When the fears are already present, in the midst of conflict, they are compounded by the fear of the conflict itself as well as the magnifying effect of the conflict on the fears which are brought into it.

Nothing works better in dealing with fear than direct, calm assurance on the part of the leader that the idea of disaster you are now anticipating is not likely to come to fruition. I recall an experience I had on a jet that lost its hydraulic system in the air, leaving it without brakes, without the mechanism to automatically lower the landing gear, and without the use of the regular controls for steering the plane. The pilot described the situation, told us what he was going to do, and then related his training to deal with such situations and implied that though this was unusual everything could be handled rather easily and simply. Instead of increasing our fear all the more, he did quite the opposite by arousing our confidence in his training, ability, and experience to deal with just such a situation as we were now experiencing. The key elements in doing this were:

    Statements of assurance that this could be handled

    A calm and relaxed demeanor and voice

    A clear description of what was happening and what it meant

    An understandable plan which was being put into effect to deal with the situation.

V

Surfacing Submerged Conflict

Perhaps as damaging to an organization's life as blatant fighting and contention is covert, underground dissention. Rumors, hidden activities, talking about people or groups "behind their backs," and work that is at cross-purposes are all symptoms of such unhealthy strife. In this situation the leader's skills and wisdom are profoundly necessary. A leader who is uncomfortable with dissention, who is unable to encourage others to express their differences, who negatively judges those who do surface disagreements is going to cause even more organizational difficulty.

As I was writing this chapter I got a phone call from a bishop about a situation in a church where the vestry (church governing body) asked for the pastor's resignation after eight months of his ministry. I had spoken with the pastor by phone on about six occasions over the last two months. I learned from him and the bishop that the pastor had had several negative and uncomfortable experiences with some of the people in the congregation. On one occasion he suggested that it would not be a good idea for one particular couple to get married. He based this on some testing that he had done with them in premarital counseling. Also, he had not done certain parts of his work and had had a rather vigorous disagreement with the organist which ended with her resignation. To hear the story from the bishop and from the pastor, the people in this congregation who are uncomfortable with the pastor had taken their grievances to one another rather than speaking directly to him. Their dissatisfaction led, after eight months, to a vestry meeting to which the pastor was not invited and then to the senior warden (chairperson of the vestry) requesting the pastor to resign. When the pastor refused to resign, the bishop was asked to come to a vestry meeting. At that meeting the pastor was asked to leave the meeting and the vestry submitted their complaints to the bishop, hoping that he would join them in their assessment that this was the wrong priest for their congregation.

The process used to manage conflict at this church is very common in organizations. The people did not tell those with whom they were dissatisfied what their problems were. Indeed, this problem was continued when the vestry and bishop asked the priest to leave. So the problems were not dealt with. Further, the leadership committee of the congregation is now trying to make a decision for the congregation without involving the larger group in any way in that decision. What is likely to happen if the pastor resigns (and especially if he lets it be known to those who support him that he was railroaded out of the job) is that those who didn't know what was happening will now be angry. They were not given a chance to have a say in the decision, and the organization will be left with a new conflict between those who felt something was put over on them and those who felt they had to make a responsible leadership decision for the congregation.

One of the things that is being said in that congregation is, "If we include others in the conversation, if we tell them what is going on and what our dissatisfactions are, it will increase the conflict; it may cause new conflicts that do not presently exist." That reasoning puts the vestry in a no-win situation because they will have that conflict if they get from the bishop what they want (i.e. pressure on the pastor to resign), and the pastor's supporters perceive that they have had no opportunity to defend him or hear the facts. On the other hand, if the vestry gets what they don't want (a recommendation for the pastor to stay) they have no experience with each other in addressing and working through difficulties.

Much of the literature on conflict management is about this problem of not surfacing directly the organization's difficulties and describes the need for confrontation as a way to combat it. What is meant by confrontation in behavioral science literature is not what the word sounds like. The word sounds like you are licensing the people in the organization to attack one another. "Let's have a confrontation meeting," has the ring of "Let's get those dirty so and so's and put them in their place." This is not what is meant by confrontation.

Invitation

In order to avoid raising fears by such confrontation labels, I use the words invitation, or acknowledgment. These words affirm the fact that differences are perceived by the various parties to the conflict, yet movement is toward seeking solutions, calling the others closer in order to work through differences, naming the difficulties, and encouraging the others to stay in the process of seeking jointly acceptable outcomes.

Encouraging the others to join with you in dealing with the conflict and encouraging the others to stay with you in the process is perhaps the single most important conflict management skill one can use. Mostly we are dealing with the issue of fear at this point, but the subordinancy issue is present as well. With regard to fear, it is important to remember that as a person's perception of powerlessness increases, the likelihood of violence or bizarre behavior increases. Those persons who perceive themselves to be powerless to affect by other means what is happening are most likely to strike out against others in destructive ways. If I am unable to get what I want by rational and fair means, then I am likely either to give up (Seligman's helplessness idea) or I am likely to strike out against what I perceive to be causing me pain, holding me back, or frustrating me in some way. Note that a greater incidence of depression and violence is among alienated powerless persons in society than among those who have opportunities to exert change and influence on the system. In my own experience the only times I have struck anyone have been when I perceived myself to be powerless to have an effect on them by rational communication patterns. It was when *I felt powerless* that I acted with bellicosity.

This knowledge should help the leader in conflict situations. If the leader is aware that increasing the ability of those with whom she is in conflict to use rational and fair means will improve their conflict management skills and lower their level of fear and frustration, then she can see that encouraging the other to stay in the process is likely to be helpful in dealing with the tension as well.

To illustrate this point further, I was recently working with a staff where a great deal of friction had developed between two second-level staff persons almost immediately after the second was hired. Al had been on the staff for six years and Bob had just come on board. Al felt that Bob was scheming with the boss to make the institution into an impersonal, legalistic bureaucracy. Bob perceived

Al to be self-centered, not wanting to learn anything, and stuck in outmoded and inefficient patterns of work. Both Al and Bob spoke with me about the conflict. As it happened Bob was more threatened by the conflict than was Al. I encouraged Al to go to Bob and invite him to talk about the problems they were having. When Bob got belligerent and called Al names, Al did not respond to the deprecations (non-reward, extinction) but asked if they could name specifically what was hurting their relationship (invitation). When, on one occasion, Bob abruptly left the meeting saying, "This is hopeless," Al waited two days and again went to Bob's office requesting that they explore the reasons for the discomfort between them, assuming that each had contributed to the difficulty, and it was not all one person's fault. This exploration was very difficult for both of them. Al was often discouraged and perceived Bob to be interpersonally incompetent, high-strung, and conspiratorial. Several times Al said to me, "I don't think it's worth it. Nothing will come of this. I am wasting my time." But Al hung in there. Bob, on the other hand, was afraid that he would lose his new job. He was utterly perplexed by the advice he was getting to level with the other person and by the regular invitations to attempt to work through the difficulties. After several invitations to work through their problems, which on the surface came to little, Bob began to feel secure enough to stay with the process of seeking solutions to problems rather than avoiding them, running from uncomfortable meetings, or attacking Al by calling him names. After a time they were able to work rather well together.

When I recommend this process to leaders, they are often nonplussed by the suggestion. After all, the other person started it, or he or she has done more damage than the person with whom I am talking, or he or she won't be able to handle such an invitation and will, inevitably, use such a show of what may be perceived to be weakness against the one who is doing the inviting. In fact, all these outcomes are possible. However, these disasters are less probable by initiating the action than by avoiding it or fighting. But even more important than this fact is the reality that you are the only one that you have charge of in any situation. You cannot control the other person; you cannot get him or her to do what you want (whether or not that person should be taking the initiative). The only person over whom you have any control is yourself, and if *you* want to deal with the conflict, *you* will have to take the initiative. If the other takes the initiative, you are lucky. If the other person doesn't take the initiative, you better do so.

Making Contact

The second thing you need to consider when you are inviting the other to join with you is "making contact." Herman and Korenich talk about contact in this way:

> When two people are in contact, they are really seeing, hearing, and experiencing each other and what is going on *right here, right now*. When you are in good contact with another person, there are minimum interferences with your sensing processes.
>
> When you are not in good contact, your senses are being interfered with—you are worrying, thinking of something other than what's going on here and now, making assumptions in your mind about what the effects of your words will be on the other person, and so on. When your mind is preoccupied, of course, it is unlikely that you are really able to use your eyes and ears, to experience what is really happening in your immediate situation.[1]

68

What happens when we are not making contact with each other is intellectualizing, playing "ain't it awful," or self-neutralizing. When one is *intellectualizing* he is generalizing or abstracting rather than talking specifically about this situation and the relationships involved. When a person is generalizing, he talks of broad categories of situations rather than what is happening right now. "What do you think a person should do when his boss doesn't give him the resources he needs to do the work?" That is generalizing. Are you talking about yourself? By "resources" do you mean money or staff? What work is it that you want to accomplish? One of the best clues to help you assess whether contact is being made is whether or not there is eye contact. Often the person who is generalizing will look at the floor, at the ceiling, or off into space rather than look at the other person.

"Ain't it awful" is listing complaints without allowing opportunity for serious discussion as to what to do about any of them.

Self-neutralization is where the individual makes a critical comment about another and then mitigates its power by trying to be fair or accurate, perhaps in order to avoid conflict or hurting the other person's feelings. "I'm not sure you are doing a very good job of inhibiting developers from buying up land in the township," one of the voters said to a planning committee member the other day, "but it must be terribly difficult to do that. Those developers are really smart, they've got a lot of staff to help them, and there are so many of them it must be impossible for you to keep track of all that is going on." Here the person says what she feels and yet fails to achieve contact because she softens the blow of the critique by "understanding the circumstances." So she is not helping the other make contact with what she is actually thinking or feeling.

Often self-neutralization is an attempt to increase empathy toward the other. Being empathetic means that you are aware of what the likely consequences of your behavior will be and have some idea of what other people's feelings might be by "standing in their shoes." However, my empathy should not interfere with my expression of myself. I can empathize with your pain, and I can share my concerns without neutralizing them. For example, "I am angry that you did not vote against the zone variance for the new housing development. You must have some feelings in this situation as well, will you tell me what they are?"

Structuring the Interaction

It is helpful when inviting the other to deal with the conflict you are facing to take some initiative to structure the process of the conversation or interaction. This is best done if it is a joint effort. In fact, it can be the first move you make toward joint problem solving. If you are able to reach agreement on how you are going to approach your difficulties, you are going to increase the probability of reaching agreement about the difficulties themselves. This can be one of those small successes that leads the way to further success in working through the problem.

Here is a process that many have found to be helpful:

First agree on the guidelines or ground rules you will use to determine whether the conflict tactics you are using are fair. I like the guidelines given by David Luecke in *The Relationship Manual*:

1. No one is allowed to define the situation for the other. Each person expresses *only* his or her viewpoint.

70

2. Space is always given for an alternative point of view.
3. Respond to the statement of the other *before* expressing your own view.
4. It is OK to disagree. You can enjoy a conversation without coming to agreement. You only need to hear, understand, and accept what the other has said as his or her point of view.

Another set of guidelines for structuring the context of the conflict are those delineated by George Bach[2]:

1. Statements are rational and realistic, not contrived and insincere, or manipulative.
2. Statements are fair; the other can cope with them and integrate them and respond; they are not devastating or impairing to the other's motivation and capacity to continue.
3. Genuine feelings are shared; persons are not detached/withdrawn for faking concern.
4. Each is willing to acknowledge a share in the conflict and its resolution means that one does not blame outside sources or the other alone.
5. Humor produces relief, not sarcasm, putdowns, or humiliation.
6. Feedback is accurate and relevant, not distorted or full of attributions.
7. Statements are clear and contain concrete details, not vague and general.
8. Statements are related to the here and now, something that you can do something about.
9. Each party is willing to be flexible and open to change.

Structuring the interaction also means that the the two of you will talk about what the literal steps will be in the development of the conversation. This will seem awkward the first time that you do it (and the second and third, but you will develop some facility with it over time). However, what you are doing by agreeing on the problem-solving process is helping everyone involved feel more in control and more powerful, and hence less likely to act crazy (again, there are no guarantees here, but we are exploring processes that can or may help). Here is a process that often works (from *The Relationship Manual*):

    A. Identify one issue that seems important to work on at a time.

    B. Take turns restating what you each want with respect to the issue and what is most important to you.

    C. One of you offers a "summary statement" of what you both have said and then ask, "Is this the way you see it?"

    D. The other agrees with the summary statement or revises it or offers additional information and another "summary statement" again checking it out. This continues until you agree on a summary statement.

    E. Whoever has the next turn now offers a proposal: I would be willing to . . . . if you would be willing to . . . .

    F. The other now responds to the offer. If you respond by accepting the offer as stated, go directly to the next step; if not, respond by offering modifications or a counterproposal, the other responds with further modification or another counterproposal until a proposal is accepted.

    G. Whoever has the next turn summarizes what you have agreed upon, emphasizing what each is getting in a positive way. The other responds with agreement (or clarification if needed) and suggests doing something to share the good feelings of working through your differences.

Problem Definitions

The other thing to be aware of as you move toward the other in conflict is the importance of the way problems or issues are defined in the first place. We block ourselves from seeing options and possibilities because of the way we describe what we see or experience. Bandler and Grinder[3] point to three problems that regularly occur as individuals try to explain the world—or describe what is the matter at the present time and how it might be corrected. Bandler and Grinder's three categories are: generalization, deletion, and distortion.

Generalization is the problem of describing something in a way that detaches the experience from the specific event and leads one to represent more of the experience in the description than is actually the case. It is useful to generalize that sharp knives can cut you, but it is not the case that all knives are sharp and therefore dangerous (as is the case with a butter knife). Generalizations as problem descriptions often start: "You always . . . . . . ," or "Everybody thinks . . . . . . ," or "People . . . ." (as in: "People are out to get me!" or "People would like to see you get another job"). Sometimes the generalization is a vague description of something that happened: "When we got to the meeting, we were surprised and frightened by the president's unprovoked attack." "Unprovoked attack" doesn't specify very much. If what exactly happened were described, it might help everyone get a better grip on the whole situation and its meaning: "When we got to the meeting, we were surprised by the president's statement that Jim had forgotten to pick him up and he had to walk to the meeting." Even if the president's statement had the tone of attack, it is still more easily dealt with by being specific. "The president was red in the face and shouted at Mary that he was angry at Jim because he had not been picked up." This tells the whole story rather than leaving to one's imagination what might have happened or what the meaning of the events might be.

Sometimes the generalization is one that attributes

more meaning to the situation than is actually there. "My boss doesn't appreciate my work" is a generalization that puts everyone in a difficult situation for problem solving. A more specific description of the situation might be: "My boss doesn't come down to my office and talk from time to time," or "My boss was unhappy with the way I handled the Fourth Street Project."

The second kind of inappropriate problem definition is what Bandler and Grinder call "deletion." Deletion is selectively paying attention to certain dimensions of experience and excluding others. Sometime this is done in quite an obvious way. "You never plan ahead" is a problem description that may ignore the fact that the person does plan meals, does manage money, does plan at work, but does not plan what to do on the weekends.

A more subtle kind of deletion is describing part of the experience but deleting the rest as in, "I'm confused." When what is meant is, "I'm confused by Tom's request for more feedback after he told me he didn't want to talk about his behavior." The first statement implies that the speaker is generally confused, confused about every-thing. The second gives full appreciation to the part of one's experience that is causing the difficulty.

Finally, some problem definitions are distortions. Distortion implies some kind of finality that may in fact not be there. Often what is being described is a process, but the process is described as if it were a conclusion or completed actuality. Thus Bandler and Grinder say the statement, "I regret my decision to return home," is a distortion, implying that the decision to return home is final. Most decisions can be changed. Regretting a decision does not allow the possibility that deciding is an ongoing process. A more accurate description is, "I regret that I am deciding to return home." Another illustration they give is, "I am surprised at her resistance to me," which is a distortion of, "I am surprised that she is resisting me." The former sentence implies that resistance is final and forever, the latter that resistance is an ongoing decision that might be changed in the future.

Because of these problems in the initial stages of confrontation or invitation, it is important that problem statements be framed in ways that help to clarify rather than obfuscate the difficulties we are trying to deal with. The more specifics put into the statement the better. Often problem statements take this form, *Who is doing or not doing what to whom?* This particular form helps the problem definer tell as much as possible, especially if it meets the criteria:

1. It describes what is problematic, what is the difference between what is and what is the desired state. It isn't very helpful to have an accurate description of what is if it is not something you want to do something about.

2. The statement is specific and descriptive, letting everyone know what happened, what is happening, or what needs to be changed.

3. The statement is not an attribution, that is, a guess about what the other intends, or thinks, or means by a given behavior or statement. "She is trying to wreck this organization" is usually an attribution, or mind reading, a guess at what the other's motives are.

4. Problem statements shouldn't be putdowns. Putdowns are different from descriptions in that their intention is to add pain to an already difficult situation.

5. Problem statements describe something that one can do something about. It is not a problem statement to describe something to which no one can respond, such as, "The problem is that it snows in Alaska." This

is not something anyone can do anything about and is, therefore, not a "workable problem."

Sometimes workable problems may be discovered by talking about and exploring a non-workable problem, e.g., the statement, "John is too big for the seat," is not workable, but the statement, "The seat is too small for John," may be workable. Changing John's size may not be within the realm of possibility, but changing contours of seats may be.

A useful technique for generating workable problem statements is for me and the person with whom I have the disagreement to make a list of workable problems rather than to try to identify just one that we can agree on. If we come up with a list of problems, we are more likely to find some that will succeed. Further, we don't get stuck in a presumption that my definition of the problem is better than your definition. A list of problems acknowledges that there are many dimensions to the problem and that working one aspect of the problem will not "solve" the whole thing. It will only give us a start into a complex situation. Two other advantages to listing problems are that the same problem can be stated in different ways suggesting different roles that individuals can take in alleviating the difficulty, and different processes by which the problems might be dealt with can be suggested. To illustrate, let's look at a situation and some of the workable problems that may be contained in it.

The 4-H rents a community building owned by the city to carry out a nutrition program. The director of the community building and the 4-H agent get into a conflict over where, when, and how the training in canning will be done. They generate this list of workable problems:

The director doesn't allow the 4-H agent to have keys to the building.

The 4-H agent did not put away the utensils used in the kitchen on three occasions.

The 4-H agent was unable to put the utensils away on these occasions because the person with the key was not in the building.

The 4-H agent wants to have the building open in the evening for canning training sessions.

The director does not have money in the budget for hiring supervisory and custodial staff for evening use of the building.

The director does not have an alternative means of funding supervisory and custodial staff for evening use of the building.

The 4-H agent does not have alternative means of staffing supervisory and custodial staff for evening use of the building.

This list illustrates that the problems are not all one-sided; each statement has problematic elements on both sides. It also illustrates the fact that a list of problems can suggest ideas about the way problems can be aproached. For example, when the 4-H agent complains about not being able to work at night, the director indicates her perceptions of what interferes with these work hours. This suggests to both of them that alternative approaches to the problem can help them address it.

When to Escalate Conflict

Up to this point in this chapter I have been describing the importance of limited escalation, or bringing problems up when they occur and helping people in the group or organization address their difficulties. However, it is not always appropriate to escalate conflict. A number of factors should be taken into account as you consider moving toward conflict escalation.

Newness. The first thing to consider is how new the relationships are in the conflict setting. People who are just getting acquainted with one another don't manage differences well. They tend to drop away very quickly, unless they have high stakes in the outcome of the conflict. I have learned through many years of teaching courses in conflict management that it is not a good idea to get a new group into conflict experiences too early. The people are just getting acquainted, and they have plenty of anxiety about what these relations are going to be like without adding the anxiety of conflict. So in the beginning of a group session I start with highly structured and safe experiences. This helps people get to know one another and helps them develop trust and a sense of security in the group which will make later risk-taking more profitable.

Skills and experience. I am also concerned about the ability of people to handle themselves in a conflict. The less skilled and less experienced people are in developing and keeping relationships the more difficult it will be for them to manage the conflict. This is also true about the issues with which they are dealing; the less they know about the subject, the more conflict is likely to get out of hand. Earlier I mentioned the impact of powerlessness and conflict. The less experience, skill, and knowledge, the more powerless the person will feel. Thus, the invitation to deal with issues must be much more cautious and gently initiated with novices than with persons who are "old hands."

Structure. This is also a critical element. The more structure there is the more the perception of safety.

The less structure there is the more confusion and possibility of discomfort. If the organization you are with has structures and processes for problem-solving and conflict management, they should be used. If not, they can easily be created on an *ad hoc* basis as the conflict develops. This creation of structure will add components of security to compensate for the components of risk that come with the conflict situation. To illustrate this, think about a conflict where no authority or agreed-on problem-solving process exists to help deal with the situation. For example, a squabble between neighbors over who gets the fruit from the limbs of a tree that hang over the property line could create more anxiety than a conflict with an auto mechanic. When you know you can go to the service representative or to the service department manager if you do not get satisfaction with the mechanic, you are likely to experience less trauma than when you have no guidelines or authorities to turn to. It is easier to deal with a conflict when there is clear policy and guidelines on how to go about it than when it is a so-called free-for-all.

Available time. As the time to work the problem decreases, the intensity of the conflict increases. It will be to the advantage of everyone to allocate ample time to work through the issues, but it is also essential to establish a time when the necessary decisions are to be made. Time pressure increases anxiety and the amount of fear present in the situation. If you want to increase pressure toward decision making, a common strategy is to set a short deadline.

Other factors that are likely to make a difference in the way people handle conflict are:

Degree of role clarity. This problem occurs when there is disagreement as to who should be making what decisions based on traditional assumptions about who has the responsibility for those decisions. This is being experienced most profoundly in marriages. Traditional role differentiation indicates that it is the husband who should make decisions about large purchases and the wife who makes decisions about food, clothing, and day-to-day maintenance items. These assumptions about who makes what decisions are being challenged in some modern marriages and changed in others. these changes increase the difficulty in making decisions and managing conflict because the traditional rules do not apply. The greater the confusion in understandings about who should make what decision, the greater the difficulty in managing the conflict.

Resource disparity. This is also a factor in conflict management. Both tangible and intangible resource disparity are factors (this language is that of John Scanzoni and Maximiliane Szinovacz in *Family Decision-Making*[4]). Tangible resource disparity has to do with the differences that can be measured, such as the amount of education the parties have, job status, or income. Intangible resource disparity has to do with self-esteem. Resource disparity relates back to that question of powerlessness that we spoke of earlier. The more I perceive myself to have fewer resources to deal with the situation, the more helpless, powerless, or violent I am likely to be. (If I can't get what I want by logical argument, perhaps I can attack you, overtly or covertly, or at least punish you even though I may not be able to accomplish my goal.) Often resource disparity is irrelevant to the actual problem being addressed. Nonetheless, the associations people have of others in their roles may affect their self-esteem and seriously handicap or mar the ability of the parties to stay with and work through the difficulties they are facing.

Third parties, audiences. Research on the effect of outsiders on conflict has been reported by Rubin and Brown[5]. Generally, audiences (whether they are invited to observe as mediators or whether they just happened to be present) have a salutary effect on conflict. Where the parties are aware that they are observed by neutral, impartial, and, presumably, objective outsiders, they tend to temper their behavior to fit the prevailing norms regarding appropriate behavior in conflict. One exception to this is when the audience is on your "team." For example, labor/management disputes are often made more difficult because the negotiators are more concerned with the perception they are giving to those they represent than with the attempt to reach an agreement with their counterparts in the bargaining. This makes compromise difficult. Another exception is when the audience is looking for blood and reveling in the difficulties that the conflicted parties are experienceing. It is not unusual for newspaper and television reporters to bait protagonists in such a way that their responses make "a good story." This, of course, is not helpful for managing differences, and the role of the reporter as impartial observer (which can be very salutary) is forsaken.

Mutuality. Scanzoni also talks about what he calls "mutuality" as a critical factor in the management of differences. Mutuality comes out of the past experiences of both parties. It has to do with past relationships between them, and the assessment that they now make concerning how cooperative, trustworthy, fair, or empathetic each is to the other's concerns. If one's assessment of the other is that he or she has not been cooperative or trustworthy, then, of course, the current difficulties will be complicated by past experience. This does not mean that agreement is impossible, only that more stipulations, more guarantees, more "inspections," as in the case of Russia and the United States, are needed before one will believe that the other can be trusted.

The leader as model in conflict settings. The way you are aware of yourself in conflict will profoundly affect your ability to manage yourself and work with others in the midst of a conflict. Freud talked about the unconscious as a part of the self of which you are not fully aware. It was his perception that below the surface of full awareness you are working out a scenario that can make sense to your non-conscious self but not always to the conscious self. Perhaps you have a wish you want to fulfill or you feel guilty about an event or an imagined event and believe, non-consciously, that you must be punished or pay for it. Freudian therapy works on the premise that as you become aware of the non-conscious drama in which you perceive yourself to be an actor, the script of the drama loses its power of control over you, and you begin to write a new script. Tom Wolfe in *The Electric Kool-Aid Acid Test* (Farrar, Straus & Giroux, 1968), refers to another person's choices and behaviors as "that's his movie." He says what Freud said before him, that the individual looks at the world and consciously and non-consciously assigns meaning, richness, (or dullness), and purpose to what is happening. This is not difficult for us to fathom at some immediately accessible levels, yet much of what is happening is only partially available to us as individuals, though it may be much clearer to others who are with us.

One man with whom I worked for four years had been in prison some years before and was now a community organizer. When I asked him why he had decided to go "straight" he said that he was tired of playing "cops and robbers." He knew what his "movie" had been and now he was choosing another. Perhaps you are aware of other dramas or movies that friends are playing out: the beautiful person who is never ruffled or affronted by anything, the big, hard-nosed boss, the devil's advocate, the realist professor. Eric Berne delighted many of us with his ability to categorize and give colorful names to many of the dramas which he called scripts, games, or injunctions, depending on the special category of life expression he was identifying.

Some of these "movies," or "scripts," or "dramas" are so much a part of our character, so hidden and protected from our usual awareness, and so important to our perceptions of what is important for survival that we cannot get close to them, let alone change them, without the help of highly trained persons in therapeutic settings. Nonetheless, much of what we experience can be changed if we become aware of it and substitute a crazy, destructive, or helpless script for one that is life-enhancing. This is what is at the heart of Norman Vincent Peale's positive thinking, W. Clement Stone's positive mental attitude, and Robert Schuller's possibility thinking. They recommend replacing a defeatest script full of ennui and nausea with a new movie of hope and success. The problem that many of us have with Peale, Stone, and Schuller is their positive movie seems too unreal—like a Disney cartoon—and doesn't face or affirm tragedy as a part of the victory of life. Rather, they seem to say that tragedy doesn't exist, that when it does occur, it is a manifestation of evil and should be avoided, shunned, denied, put away.

A different kind of movie affirms the conflict and tragedy of life as part of what is real and finds within it opportunities for enpowerment, change, growth, and stimulation. What has made the great leaders of the world notable is not the absence of conflict or struggle from the implementation of their leadership—just the opposite—greatness has come from the way they addressed adversity. Who remembers the leaders during the times of quiet and peace? Few. From where did those we most admire come? They came, like Ghandi, from the struggle to free a captive nation from the rule of another; they came, like Roosevelt, from a war against economic depression and the attempted tyranny of other nations; they came, like Margaret Sanger, from a war against women's ability to control what happens to their bodies; and they came, like Susan Anthony, from a war to deny suffrage to women.

What was the movie of Sanger, Ghandi, Roosevelt, or Anthony? It was not the movie of helplessness, nor was it the movie of annihilation of the enemy.

"Well," you say, "that's all great for Ghandi and Sanger, but for me, no way. I've neither the ability nor the temperament to invite conflict or to stay in it. I'd rather be at peace and get along with everybody." When you say this, are you aware of the movie you're in? It's *Dick & Jane Go to Uncle Bob's Farm*. Nothing really happens in this script. In fact its essence is the lack of action. This is not the movie I choose if I believe that I have free will, if I believe I have something to give that makes a difference to someone and that I have some control over what I do.

Recently I spoke with a woman who is the new director

of a community action agency. She said she wanted to make significant changes in the way the program had been run—such as letting some people go who were not pulling their weight, moving the main office, and dropping some ineffective programs. The man who used to be the director of the agency is now her supervisor. Her recommended changes threatened him, so he encouraged her to keep doing as he had done in that position. At first he only made recommendations, then he sent strong memos threatening her if she didn't do as he said, and finally he told other people that she was incompetent and made up stories about her.

His behavior was threatening to the new director. She was annoyed, scared, angry, and confused all at once. But her picture of herself was of a person with good ideas who listens to others and who stands up to attack no matter how petty, personal, or peevish it is. (Notice I said "stands up to attack" not "dishes out the same meat she gets.") This internal stance comes through. Everybody understands it—not immediately, not in the same way, not always clearly—but somehow it is perceived by superiors in the organization, by her antagonist, and by other observers that she has integrity (which means "wholeness"). It is through her struggle with this adversary that her true mettle is revealed. Most of the observers come to respect her and realize that she can "manage" tough situations.

The power of this kind of leadership is twofold. Part of the power is in the long-term effects it has on the decisions being made—where the office will be, who stays on the staff, and what the program will be—and the other part of the power is the profound effect it has on others who see a new movie and believe it could be a model for them. If the top leaders of the organization choose other movies, they befuddle, confuse, antagonize, drive people away from taking responsibility for themselves, and lose their impact on the rest of the organization.

VI

How the System and Environment Affect Conflict Management

Conflict is more than a function of interpersonal dynamics. Much of what shapes conflict and starts it in the first place has to do with factors that are beyond the interaction of individual personalities. Some conflict is structured into the fabric of an organization. In the government of the United States this is called checks and balances. A built-in conflict, for example, is structured into the differentiation of the legislature in two forums, the House and the Senate. And each of those bodies is divided in two groups, Republicans and Democrats. In each case the loyalties of the representatives are designed to be different—the members of the House loyal to smaller, presumably more homogeneous constituencies than the members of the Senate who are loyal (or responsible to) more diverse, broader constituencies. And each of the parties have different identities and constituencies which they represent. The conflict, which emerges out of the differences built into the system, is a natural, expected (indeed, wanted) confrontation that is supposed to diminish collusion, group-think, and bossism.

However, the structured differentiation of constituencies and loyalties is not the only so-called systemic factor that affects the shape of conflict in organizations. Other important factors are: the norms of the group, the roles of the participants, the procedures used to do problem solving, the presence of audiences, group size, and the physical characteristics of the site where the conflict is taking place.

Norms. Perhaps norms are the most important factors of all those listed. Norms are necessary to group life, because they are a part of the glue that holds society together. Norms are the unwritten rules that people abide by in order to function as a group. By and large, people are not fully conscious of the norms that shape their behavior, unless they are infringed upon or challenged. For example, it used to be the norm in North American society to use masculine gender pronouns to refer to both sexes when describing people in general. To have used the feminine gender to refer to all people would have been considered incorrect and would have been changed by an editor or would have become a reason for derision if a speaker had used the word "womankind" when all the human race was meant.

Norms not only prescribe appropriate behavior, but they also have sanctions associated with them. That is, if one infringes on the proper functioning prescribed by the norms of a given group certain punishment will be brought to bear against the misconduct. If no sanctions are brought to bear when one does not conform to the usual practice, we do not say that a norm is broken but that a behavior pattern has changed. A behavior pattern is a norm without sanctions. A norm is an (usually) unwritten rule to which sanctions are brought to bear when the rule is broken. Thus, if you are the only male in a restaurant not wearing a tie and nothing is said by the management or other patrons, you have not broken a norm, though you have not conformed to the behavior pattern.

Norms profoundly affect the progress of conflict,

beacuse in most organizations these agreed-upon un-written laws of behavior have powerful sanctions. Sometimes the norms associated with conflict are not helpful—in fact, destructive—of processes of healthy conflict management. For example, some organizations have norms that prohibit direct sharing of differences with those in conflict. Those who challenge publicly the leadership of the president or raise "embarrassing" questions in meetings are considered to be troublemak-ers. They are told that if they have a problem they should do their best to get along with others. If they must challenge what others are doing, they should do so in private, but never raise questions on the floor of public meetings. Direct sharing is troublemaking; public shar-ing is behaving like an agitator.

Many organizations have norms opposed to the existence of any conflict. Conflict or difference is seen to be a sign of failure; it is something to be feared and avoided or put down. Because of the norms that exist about conflict, strong remedial action is immediately taken to guarantee that no conflict at all occurs within the organization. When it does, those who cause it must either leave or conform. This norm, of course, does not exist in all organizations, but is true of many volunteer groups and becomes a serious problem for them.

Those organizations that have norms supporting healthy and fair conflict usually have sanctions which punish those who do *not* raise differences when they have them and which set limits on the kind of behavior that is appropriate within the conflict. For example, I worked with a church in a large city where a small group of people opposed the recommendations of a planning committee. They acted out their opposition by talking only with their friends and those they thought would agree with them and by spreading rumors about the intentions of the members of the planning group. When he heard of this rump group, the pastor called their behavior to the attention of the governing board and invited several persons who were key leaders of the opposition to make public statements about their concerns. As a part of his encounter with the dissenters, he made it clear that sneaky and covert behavior broke the norms of that church which had a long history of honoring diversity and difference. Thus, in that situation difference was embraced, rather than shunned.

It is important that these unhealthy conflict norms be challenged and changed because they severely interfere with healthy problem solving and group development. At the psychological level the greater the perception of conflict, the greater the fear that is likely to be present within the organization. And, as we have seen from earlier chapters, anxiety and fear of conflict make the management of difference very difficult. On the organizational level, norms that inhibit conflict do not rid the organization of tension, they only put it out of effective reach. When you put fear of conflict together with norms that prohibit its expression, you get a double dose of problems. This double trouble keeps the organization in turmoil longer, makes the members feel less able to control themselves and their organization, and increases the likelihood of an explosion of blaming, attacking, and getting rid of.

The best way to change conflict norms in organizations is to help the people identify what their conflict norms are. Let me describe for you a process I recently used with a group of executives who were in conflict with one another. I began by explaining what organization norms were and how sanctions are associated with them in the group's life. I then gave them a list of norms I saw operating in another system with which they were all familiar. (I find it is not helpful to list the norms that are present in their system. I want them to do their own work in identifying norms rather than copying my list.) I then divided the group into small groups of six each and asked them, first, to identify all the norms they could think of that related to conflict in their organization, and second, to identify the ones that were helpful to conflict management and those that were not helpful. Each group came up with a list of about ten. When these were shared with the total group, I asked everyone to choose approximately five of the non-helpful norms they thought should be changed immediately. The group named eight! We took these eight norms and assigned each one to a different small group whose members were asked to come up with new norms to replace the old, non-helpful ones. Each group was also asked to identify new sanctions that would be appropriate if the new norms were not followed.

All the groups came up with new norms and a list of sanctions. They all agreed that the most important change was the change in the old norm: if you have a problem with the person with whom you are working do not tell that person. The new norm, of course, was exactly the opposite: if you have problems with anyone, you must tell that person what is bothering you. The sanctions they came up with were these: if a person complains to someone outside of his or her shop about his or her partner, the person who receives the complaint will (a) encourage that person to talk over the problem with the partner, (b) will indicate a willingness to go with the complainer to the partner if the complainer seems reluctant to act, (c) will follow up with the complainer to

91

see that the complaint has been addressed, and (d) will confront the complainer with his or her noncompliance with the norm.

So what the process was for changing norms was:

Identify the norms

Identify the norms you want to change

Brainstorm a list of new norms to take the place of the old norms

Choose new norms to use

Identify sanctions that will be brought to bear for noncompliance

Make sure that enforcement of the new norms is immediate after each violation

Roles. Role conflict is another type of difficulty that may arise as much from the structure of the system as from the predilections of the personalities involved. Some roles build conflict into the relationships people have with one another. For example, the role of a treasurer is to conserve and appropriately account for the disbursement of funds and the role of the research and development department is to explore new fields, dream up new ideas, and determine whether those ideas are feasible. These two roles have built-in conflict. Each one moves in a direction that is likely to cause the other a problem.

It is not always the case that the role conflict is "built in," so to speak. Sometimes individuals have different role expectations because of their backgrounds or experiences in other organizations. It is not uncommon in a voluntary organization, for example, for members of the governing board to perceive their role as one of overseeing or policy making. The staff and others, however, may believe that the governing board should be a "working board," that is, a group of people who not only tell others what to do and not do, but also implement some of the work themselves. In the literature on role conflict this is identified as conflict between the role sender (staff) and the role receiver (board member), each of whom have a different understanding of what is to be done by the role receiver.

Where the basis of the conflict comes from differing expectations about what should be done, a role clarification meeting can often help. The model for a role clarification meeting suggested by William G. Dyer in his book, *Team Building*[1], begins with the person or persons involved in the role conflict, or affected by the conflict, coming together in a meeting. At this time everyone who is affected by the problem writes answers to the following questions:

What does the organization expect of the person in this role?

What expectations do you have for others that affect performances in this role?

What do you perceive is now actually being done in that role?

What difficulties or concerns do you have about what is or is not being done in this role?

The answers to these questions are listed on newsprint and the group joins in a discussion of the various expectations, modifying them as they go along and seeking to get agreement on one item at a time.

After completing the agreements the role receiver writes a summary of the roles that have been defined. Dayal and Thomas[2] say this summary should include: (*a*) a set of activities classified as to the prescribed and discretionary elements of the role, (*b*) the obligation of the role to each role in the set, and (*c*) the expectations of this role from others in its set. These three items provide a comprehensive understanding of each individual's "role space." The written role profile is then reviewed at a subsequent meeting.

Procedures. Sometimes procedures for doing work or problem solving in groups are themselves provocators of conflict in organizations. Usually, it is because the procedures are unclear, poorly carried out, or contradictory. These difficulties should be worked out rather easily. The trick is to identify the fact that you have a procedural problem and do something about it. A wise leader will check in the midst of conflict to see if procedures are part of the difficulty confronting the group.

One group with which I worked had a procedural problem: the governing board did not tell others when they responded to complaints brought to it by staff or members. Thus, the complainants didn't know if they were being taken seriously. Another group had no procedures or mechanism for people to bring complaints or problems to the attention of the management of the organization, so each time a question was raised it was perceived as an affront to the whole organization rather than just a problem to be dealt with easily and routinely.

Usually procedural difficulties can be worked out rather simply and with the agreement of those who are not getting what they want or need when the procedural system is "fixed."

Group Size. The size of the group will affect the organization's abilities to manage conflict. As a rule of thumb, I assume that the larger the group, the more difficult it will be to understand the complexities of any given problem. When people speak to large groups they tend to simplify and dichotomize problems into binary understandings. This tendency works to the detriment of problem-solving in an organization. Important problems are rarely simple. When they are, it is a gift for which to be greatly thankful, but it is indeed rare.

In large group meetings speakers are likely to oversimply in order to be understood and make their points forcefully. This may do a lot for "revving up" the audience, but it does not provide an opportunity for responding to complex issues in a meaningful way—nor is it fair to all parties concerned.

One of the things I do as a consultant is to divide the group into smaller, more manageable groups to help individuals utilize their good sense and their natural tendencies for bonding and good relationships. These then function for the good of the whole. In a large group a person tends to feel anonymous and to lose his or her unique identity. After dividing a large group into a number of study groups, I have found it helpful to have them report their findings in writing (usually on newsprint) so that they can approach the problem in more rational, thoughtful, and humane ways.

To illustrate: I had a contract with a church in the Midwest. The church members got into a conflict when the worship committee recommended to the congregation that the furniture be changed in the sanctuary. This idea was presented at a congregational meeting held on a weekday evening. People who spoke at this meeting were adamant pro or con and were the only ones who had one clear opinion with which they battered the rest. When people left the meeting, they were frightened, confused, and angry. They felt they were not understood and were being pushed around by others who "didn't understand the real issues." We dealt with this situation by setting up a number of study groups which met four nights, once a week, for a month. These meetings were structured to help people get acquainted with one

95

another as persons first. They then were able to talk about the importance and meaning of worship in their lives. Outside experts were brought in to talk about the complexity of the issues involved from a variety of points of view, and the people were given a chance to pull together statements that described their consensus about what they hoped would be good for the church. Thus, the progression of the discussion was toward finding out what is best for the organization, rather than pushing for what is best for me or my group. We encouraged participation in small groups so that all would have a chance to hear and be heard in an environment of support rather than in an environment of fear and acrimony.

Physical Characteristics of the Site. An important environmental factor in shaping the progress of conflict and, perhaps, helping initiate it is the arrangement of people in the environment where the conflict is taking place. One good way to help redirect the conflict from a disagreement between factions to a disagreement with the leader is to put the two factions together in a typical audience format with the leader "up-front." This configuration fosters challenging the leader rather than dealing with the issues between the groups.

Keeping the groups separate and limiting communication between them reduce opportunities for clarification and genuine understanding and increase fantasies about what the other thinks and intends.

Of course, rooms where the acoustics are poor and people are uncomfortable add to the tension, because these conditions set up stress reactions in the individuals, compounding their fear and increasing the probability of inappropriate responses.

Other physical factors which inhibit quality conflict management are:

Not looking at the person you are talking or listening to

Putting one person or group in a prestige or power position relative to the other (in larger chairs, behind desks, on raised daises)

Meeting on one group's turf (not meeting on neutral ground)

Meeting late at night when people are very tired.

In summary, not all the causes of conflict are issues or interpersonal relations. The conditions in the organization and the environment can also add to the group's tension. The site itself, procedures, norms, and group size are factors that you the leader need to understand, if not control.

VII

Curbing Conflict

It is obvious that many times conflict must be de-escalated. Conflict is not always good for an organization and can be harmful to organizational life. Sometimes individuals engage in behavior that is destructive to themselves or to others; sometimes the conflict consumes so much of the group's attention and energy that little is left over to accomplish the group's mission. Let's begin by identifying those situations when conflict should be de-escalated.

Meetings become "shouting matches" where individuals are unable to make full and complete statements of their opinions or ideas.

Factions or individuals do not take into account the good of the organization and the other factions but consider only their own point of view and commitment.

Fear is so high that members are immobilized; they do not attend meetings, don't respond to letters or phone calls, or leave discussions when certain subjects come up.

Blaming, scapegoating, attacking become the order of the day.

The costs of the conflict are too high: time, money, and resources spent on the conflict are beyond the organization's means.

Some people perceive themselves to be devastated and leave the organization.

Some people or groups are engaged in such destructive behavior as: sabotaging other groups' plans and activities, defacing property, physically striking other persons, leaking organization secrets to outsiders.

Such are the characteristics of situations needing de-escalation. De-escalation does not mean the absence of difference or conflict. De-escalation means that the challenges raised by the various parties involved are fair—are kept within certain bounds. This is not to say that there are to be no win/lose struggles—sometimes there will be. It is not to say there will be no confrontation—sometimes there must be. The conflict, win/lose, must be engaged, but it must be kept within bounds, like a boxing match—a winner and loser will be declared, but the process will be kept fair.

How does one de-escalate from an out-of-control or nearly out-of-control fight to a fair conflict-management process? Of course, you cannot control the behavior of others. They will do what they will do. But you can control yourself and contribute to an environment that invites the other into fair and reasonable discourse. One of the techniques that works well is to point out to the other and to yourself what is happening. This is not always easy to do and is especially difficult without blaming or inferring blame on the other. *Just describe what you see going on.*

For example, I once was working with a pastor and two factions of a congregation. In my report to these people I stated that the pastor had verbally attacked some people in the church. The pastor was very angry with me because I did not write about what the people whom he had "attacked" had done. After he read my report, I walked into a room where he was and said good morning to him and others, but he did not respond. After a few moments I asked him a question and at first I got a cold shoulder, then a grumble, and then a blast, "What you did was terribly unfair. I thought you were a professional. You let me down. I'll never trust you again."

I replied, "You are clearly upset and very angry. Your tone, your blazing eyes, and your clenched fists say to me you are furious. You have implied I have not behaved professionally. You say I am not being fair."

"You're damn right," he replied and then went on with a speech into which I was unable to inject a thought, defense, correction, or apology. I waited for him to expel as much as he could, then said, "You have had a lot to say, and your speech has not allowed me to reply. I'd like to explain."

I continued by describing what was going on, concluding by telling him what I would like to do. The description of what was happening helped both of us stay in the here and now, look at our behavior, and decide what to do about it.

Instead of being captured by the fear, the anger, the frustration, I was stating what was happening so both of us could focus on what was manageable rather than on what was becoming unmanageable. I was inviting both of us to explore the next steps rather than for him to continue his tirade or me to start one.

There are times, of course, when one gets caught up in

the anger and responds in kind. The response of describing what is happening is still appropriate. Had I been so caught up, after venting my anger I might come to my senses and say, "We both have been shouting at each other; neither has given the other an opportunity to make his case; we have been piling argument on argument, but going in circles."

After the description of what is going on make the statement of the invitation. "I'd like to approach this in another way. Can we find a process to address our problems that will help us de-escalate a situation that seems to be out of control?" The invitation is to sanity, to order, to process, to moving slowly.

In addition to telling yourself and the other person what is happening in a conflict situation, *pay equal attention to how you proceed and to what the issues are.* This is the key to curbing conflict that is getting out of hand. The following is a list of items that will be of value in de-escalating, or at least attempting to de-escalate, the conflict:

Establish boundaries

Structure the process

Search together for common goals

Respond to threats with descriptions and statements of
    your position, not with threats

Bring in a third party or an authority

Establishing Boundaries. Two kinds of boundaries can be established to help manage the differences. One we discussed in an earlier chapter, agreeing on ground rules by which the conflict will be dealt with. The other has to do with boundaries between the warring parties so as to limit their contact. This tactic is a last resort because it does little to help reconciliation. I sometimes call this kind of boundary setting "partitioning." In partitioning each agrees that the other needs to have "space" in which to work or exist within the same system, and each agrees he or she will not invade the other's territory. Thus, various kinds of moratoriums can be established to lessen the friction between the parties. It can be agreed that each will have his or her territory which will not be invaded by the other, and a certain amount of time will be allowed to elapse before contact is again attempted. Further, rather than change the whole organization's direction or purpose, new committees or groups can be established to work on projects that the organization heretofore has not been engaged in.

When two separate programs of an organization are established to do much the same thing, but by different individuals, partitioning might occur so that both groups can carry out their tasks without interaction. Thus, for many years the attempt was made in some communities to have separate, but equal, school systems for blacks and whites. In Quebec a variety of school systems still exist for different religious groups. They are all funded by the government. Instead of arriving at decisions that make it possible for one system to meet the needs of all persons, separate, parallel systems are established. This partitioning diminishes the whole, and the separate parts may not be equal, but it may function as a temporary alternative to fighting.

Structuring the Process. This means that all the parties who are affected by the conflict participate in agreeing on who will be involved in what stages of the decision making as it develops. The parties seek to reach agreement on who will be involved in the sharing of information, who will vote (or make the final decision), how long each step will take, and the date by which the final decision will be made.

In a conflict between two persons this is often done by agreeing on an amount of time for each person to make his or her case and for the other to reply. We discussed such a negotiation process in chapter 5.

In groups the process can be made more formal by holding hearings to get all the information. This is followed by formal decision-making processes. The "hearing" can be like those that are held by the House or the Senate or they can be a debate which precedes the voting as in Roberts Rules of Order.

Common Goals. This tactic has value in those situations where it is possible for the participants to address themselves to superordinate goals and values that bind them together before they address the specifics of the conflict. In effect, what one is trying to do here is help the participants see what they have in common that is more important than the areas of conflict. It is quite difficult, usually, to get people to take this intervention seriously. It is as if the parties to the conflict are mesmerized by the pain and the immediate issues that surround (or support) the pain. Calling their attention to something that binds them together rather than looking at that which pulls them apart is a difficult task.

The need to look at those areas which bind folks together must be appreciated by all the parties. Sometimes you must wait until the level of pain gets high enough for people to be ready to try activities other than attacking and blaming to resolve their differences. I have found it possible on occasion to raise the level of pain that people are experiencing in order to help them address and appreciate the fundamental forces that hold them together rather than to look only at those forces which pull them apart. Pointing out to the other what this situation is and what the consequences of continued conflict are sometimes is enough to get the other to join in a serious look at the difficulties that are being experienced or are imminent. Talking about the costs of not managing the conflict might be an effective ploy in this situation.

Responding with Descriptions Rather Than Threats. Threats or the creation of fear of retaliation has little to recommend it in the realm of conflict management. Generating fear and attempting to convince others by posturing and threatening that you might do something if they do something and showing off your capability to harm only convinces others that you are likely to do something stupid.

No evidence has convinced me that threat of capital punishment diminished so-called "capital" crimes. Nor is there any evidence from the experience of the great nations of this world that possession of a nuclear bomb increases capacity to resolve or manage conflict. The *threat of attack* from the other only escalates fear and makes it more difficult for the parties involved to assess their situation and appropriate responses rationally. As threats increase on all sides the opposition digs its defenses in even more strongly.

Take the example of our friends who had a dog that made messes on their neighbor's lawn. The response of the neighbor whose lawn was messed on was to threaten the dog owner with death to his dog if the animal trespassed again. This did not motivate the dog owner to take more actions to control his dog (he had already taken many). It motivated him to go to his attorney and to the police to complain about his neighbor's threats and to get several persons to provoke the neighbor to make the provocative statements again so they could be witnesses if anything happened to the dog. As can be clearly seen, in this case threats led only to more trouble, not to amelioration of difficulties.

The rule is that fear begets fear, threats beget confusion. One should not assume that threats lead to a managed peace. It seems that responding to threats in kind is "natural"; it seems to be what is expected—"an eye for an eye, a tooth for a tooth." The problem is that this "natural" response is almost always against nature. That is, it moves the participants toward chaos, rather than toward oneness.

This position does not mean that you should be passive, nor does it mean that you should be weak in the face of threats from others. Stopping aggression is appropriate, defense is appropriate. But what is more likely to keep order and to diminish fear is inviting the other into a problem-solving stance. Most respected are those who have the capacity for defense but do not find it necessary to flaunt it.

What I am saying is that it is important to have the capacity to defend oneself when necessary but people should not threaten others with the use of force. Usually de-escalation is accomplished by moving toward the other rather than away. Seek to *encourage* (rather than dis-courage) the other to join you.

Third Parties. Finally, you should keep before you the possibility of bringing in an authority or third party to help with the conflict resolution. Third parties can function as an objective audience for the diminution of hostile and escalating behaviors. The third party is likely to be one toward which all the actors will seek to express their best behavior. Their presence calls forth better conflict management many times on the part of the persons who are involved. Usually the third party will help slow down the process, make sure it's fair, help establish ground rules, and will keep bringing the people who are in conflict together seeking decisions on the conflicted matters.

VIII

Advocacy or When to Encourage Conflict

Up to this point I have written mostly about curbing, controlling, and working through conflict. Sometimes, however, the leader will want to consider advocacy or be the instigator of conflict for the good of the organization and the people in it. Here are five important reasons conflict should be escalated rather than decreased:

1. People are so caught up in being nice and agreeable that they do not look seriously or are are not challenged by ideas. Instead of taking a hard look at proposals that may take a lot of energy and money, or may be risky, no one thinks to challenge or seriously review ideas as they come to the attention of the group.

2. People, wanting harmony and peace, make it difficult for anyone who is not like them to become a part of the organization. Homogeneity equals harmony or harmony equals homogeneity. Hence there is a studied oneness that comes from the emphasis on what makes them alike. Difference is not appreciated, tolerated, or understood; instead it is feared.

3. The more difference and uniqueness are accentuated the less aggressive people tend to be. Yes, it is a paradox; the more they get in touch with and honor my differences, the less they need to combat anything which challenges it. Two researchers have written about this. The first was Philip Zimbardo who wrote, "Conditions that reduce a person's sense of uniqueness, that

minimize individuality, are the wellsprings of antisocial behaviors, such as aggression, vandalism, stealing, cheating, rudeness, as well as general loss of concern for others. Conversely, prosocial behaviors are encouraged by environmental and interpersonal conditions which enhance one's sense of recognition and self-identity."[1]

Harvey Hornstein reports other intriguing support of this hypothesis:

> Harvard University has a carefully developed file of information covering over two hundred different cultural groups. The information is arranged by interest categories such as housing, clothing, and welfare, and also by each cultural group. Thus, it is possible to compare several cultural groups on a given category, or one cultural group on several categories. R. I. Watson used this file in order to further explore the relationship between deindividuation and aggression. He first sorted cultural groups according to their aggressiveness. Groups that take prisoners for the purpose of torture, particularly bloodthirsty sacrifice, and groups that engage in headhunting, or fights to the death, were scored as relatively high in aggressiveness. Those that eschewed these behaviors by keeping prisoners slaves, or by ending fights before all the enemy was killed, were scored as being comparatively low in aggressiveness.
>
> These same cultural groups were then sorted according to their degree of deindividuation. Groups employing rituals which lessened identifiable personal characteristics by causing a person to "not be himself" were scored as being high in deindividuation. Body paint, face masks, uncustomary hairdos and special war clothing (excluding armor) were all considered ways of achieving deindividuation. The pattern of aggressive and deindividuating groups that emerged was fascinating. Eighty percent of the cultural groups that deindividualized their members were also highly aggressive as compared to only 12.5 percent of the non-deindividualizing cultural groups.[2]

4. Further, in moderate amounts, conflict is a way of expressing aggression. Otherwise it might come out in such unhealthy modes as displacement, explosion, or other indirect forms, such as reaction formation or repression.

5. Finally, conflict increases consciousness, aliveness, and excitement. It wakes folks up, it keeps them on their toes. It enlivens and challenges. Without some challenge and difference organizations and relationships would become dull, constricted, and apathetic—in short, boring. Some anxiety, in other words, facilitates adjustment. It leads to striving; it stimulates learning. Soldiers in the field must have some tension to keep them alert; if they had none, they would let down their guard and their readiness.

Not all the reasons for allowing or encouraging conflict are for the organization's health or stimulation. Sometimes advocacy becomes the means by which you will lead others to take sides with you because you believe that what you have to do is just and because you are being resisted by others you perceive to be misinformed or unjust. Therefore, some conflict will come from you when you choose to advocate a position you believe to be just and necessary for the good of the group.

Don't be surprised if your advocacy generates resistance or more resistance than you had anticipated. That is the nature of challenge, it seems to generate a backlash. The two sides of human beings (the one that seeks change and challenge and the one that seeks homeostasis) seem to be incarnated quickly in organizational manifestations and as the move toward change increases, the move toward keeping things the same seems to respond in equal weight, if not even more powerfully.

What advice do I have for the leader seeking to

109

advocate a position or point of view in the organization?

First, *maintain a data base.* That is, make sure that your primary targets are substantive issues: values, goals, facts, methods. Directing your advocacy against persons will usually turn out to be counterproductive, for as you seek to discredit others their attention will be turned on you as a person rather than on the issues to be addressed.

Second, *keep all parties participating.* Some will drop out because of their aversion to conflict and their fears associated with it. Keeping your opposition with you (that is, present, not necessarily on your side) will keep your advocacy directed at issues rather than at persons and it will show that you have the good of the organization in mind (not just winning) as you approach your differences. It is fascinating to watch this important dynamic at work at political conventions. The challenge is always to get the best candidate for the job, say president of the United States, but almost never at the expense of party loyalty. Losers are expected to stay with the nominee and endorse him no matter how bitter the battle had been before the vote. This model is an excellent paradigm for the kind of conflict management proposed in this book. People are expected to contend mightily for their position, but once the decision is made they are not to "jump ship," but are now to work for the candidate who won. In order for all factions to keep participating it is incumbent on the winners (or potential winners) to challenge their opponents yet not push them so hard that should they lose their will to stay in the conflict and quit participating. The struggle cannot be an ultimate win/lose struggle for the ultimate goal is *unity* not *separation.*

Third, *when you decide as a leader to be an advocate don't push harder or faster than the system can assimilate.* This

110

usually means you can push harder than the majority of members are going to be comfortable with, but discomfort is not the sign of pushing too hard. Leaving and threatening to leave are signs of pushing too hard.

Fourth, *start small and pick your terrain with care.* Do not attempt to advocate something you know little or nothing about and be sure that you choose the area where you will engage the decision-making task. Your turf is better than the other's turf, a known opponent is easier to deal with than an unknown.

Fifth, *reinforce success and abandon failure.* "Simple-minded advice," you say. Of course, but it is easier said than done. Reinforcing success means that when you make allies for the position you are advocating, do your best to keep them with you, supporting your position. It means that you keep arguments and ideas that seem to attract adherents and help those already committed to stay with you and you drop arguments (or allies) that do not garner support, turn people off, or do not strengthen your supporters.

Finally, *maintaining so-called "second strike capability" is an important advocacy strategy.* Many leaders have only one shot in their advocacy cannon. Once it is sent forth there is no backup weapon or reloading. No matter what happens, success or failure, the one-shot advocate has nothing left but the hope that "things" will work out for the best.

A consultant can help the advocate plan for contingencies by suggesting that he or she look at probable consequences of each intervention and then plan what will be done to deal with each one. This approach can greatly enhance the advocate's staying power in a conflict, because it does not assume immediate success or failure—rather it assumes a complicated world which demands thoughtful attention through a variety of contingencies. Thus, one's motivation to continue, to stay with it, is not decimated by one failure or awkward turn of events.

IX

Self-Defense

Though it has been said many times that "the best defense is a good offense," this is not always true. When you turn from defending yourself to attacking the other person, you are esclating the conflict and probably making it more difficult to handle—both for yourself and for the other person.

You may feel justified by this response—after all, look what has been done to you. Perhaps your attack will put the other on the defensive, you reason, and he or she may not come after you. However, the research on the dynamics of conflict show this reasoning is probably fallacious. Attacks confirm the other's stereotypes of you and motivate further retaliation.

A defensive conflict management strategy should be much like the overall strategy we have been emphasizing throughout this book: *invite the other (even a person who is attacking you) to join you in a common search to identify what the problems are, stay with the other in order to work through the differences, look for alternatives that you both can agree have merit and value for each of you.*

What does working through mean? It can be diagramed in this way:

THREE PROBABLE STRATEGIES

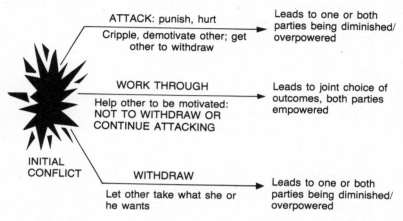

ATTACK: punish, hurt
Cripple, demotivate other; get other to withdraw

Leads to one or both parties being diminished/ overpowered

WORK THROUGH
Help other to be motivated: NOT TO WITHDRAW OR CONTINUE ATTACKING

Leads to joint choice of outcomes, both parties empowered

INITIAL CONFLICT

WITHDRAW
Let other take what she or he wants

Leads to one or both parties being diminished/ overpowered

As advocate or as defendant the same alternatives are before you. The primary difference between the two is how you perceive who initiated the conflict. "Who started it, however, is usually moot to the point of being silly, frequently impossible to answer, and more often than not, unimportant. Such questions should be dropped from one's repertoire. Even if you are able to pin the blame on one party, you still must find a way to work through the difficulties. Blaming someone else still leaves you at the same starting point unless the party "who started it" is willing to take all the blame and apologize (in other words, make a winner out of one and a loser out of the other).

Here are some dos and don'ts to consider when you are involved in a conflict and are the target of another's aggression or assertions:

In the early stages of conflict *avoid sitting down and writing out your side of the story.* Statements that you write without the assistance of others who are involved in the conflict tend to be defensive and often are not a good defense. Usually such statements contain too much, are too long, do not show the difference between that which is important and that which is trivial, and are seen by others (including your supporters) as proof of what is the matter with you.

In the position of the defender, if you feel assertive urges welling within, you will be well advised to build a case *for* your position rather than against the other. *Instead of attacking the other's arguments, look for ways to make a case for what you have been doing well and stand firmly on your record.* Keep current and keep moving toward bringing the differences into the public realm rather than going underground. Here is an example of what I am talking about: in a township not far from where I live, the supervisor was accused of administrative malfeasance by those who disagreed with his ideology. It was said that he didn't care at all about his constituents, that he had fired people without cause, and that he didn't spend enough time working for township concerns. The supervisor could have responded point by point to the charges raised by his detractors. However, to have done so would have clearly been dancing to the malignor's tune. Poor responses are "I did not," or "You're full of prunes," or "I *do* care about people. I went to ask the Widow Smith if she needed help; I *did* have cause when I fired the secretary; she didn't know how to spell. I work very hard; here is a list of my hours on the job for the last two weeks." A better response is: "This is what is going on now. Here are the results of my work [rather than look how hard I am trying]. This is the philosophy out of which I work, and here is what I intend to accomplish."

Keeping public means that all sides are informed about what is going on. It is rarely to the advantage of anyone to hold secret meetings or to keep confidential the proceedings of certain boards. This just heightens anxiety and makes it more difficult to work through conflict issues and relationships. Confidentiality increases the amount of fear in the system. If we believe that we cannot share what is going on in a meeting or in a conflict, the secretive aura enhances rather than diminishes assessments of just how dangerous this situation is. *The more that is shared, the more that is talked about, the less threatening the experience.* In addition to reducing the level of perceived threat, sharing concerns with others can help everyone see the issues that the group is facing. Support from friends is not possible if they are not informed of your straits, nor can it be effective if they are informed, but told it is supposed to be "confidential," for they can do nothing about it.

I can't say enough about the problems of confidentiality in organizational settings. In my experience the norms of confidentiality are serious barriers to managing conflict. Secrets inhibit rather than open up communication, secerets raise fear, secrets keep out people who might be able to help, secrets presume that truth will enslave rather than set one free, secrets are often lies that keep the accused from confronting them because he or she supposedly doesn't know the "charges."

I do not wish to impugn the motives of those who want to keep secrets for the sake of the "accused," feeling that conflict or questions raised about a person's leadership might besmirch a character or spoil a career. For most persons in North American society, however, the question is not *whether* one has been involved in conflict, but how one handles the conflicts that he or she is in.

116

Not giving one the opportunity to deal with the questions, the tension, the difference, or the difficulty is simply another attack on the person. This presumes incompetence to respond appropriately to the occasion or assumes that one's challenges are so weak that they cannot stand the light of public exposure and discussion.

A piece of advice that I often give pastors who are under siege from battlesome laypeople is that they *respond to challenges by affirming the value of raising criticisms,* that they even thank their scrappy board members for surfacing concerns that couldn't have been dealt with if they had not brought them up at this time. Once the others are affirmed (remember they raise their questions and concern out of the same kind of fear you are likely to have as the one under attack), ask everyone who has information about the subject in question give as much as they have—in other words, ask for the evidence against you.

You'll need to know what the ground is that you're walking on, where the others are coming from, what is going on. Without full disclosure, you'll be at a disadvantage, especially when surprise information crops up as you move along in the problem-solving process.

It is appropriate to *respond with your perception of what is happening, statements of what you want in the situation, and descriptions of your feelings.* Keep moving in a way that invites the others to share, but at the same time assumes that you are going to maintain fully your power, rights, and responsibilities in the situation.

Don't paint yourself into a corner. Some people in conflict move in a way that shows they believe that they have no options. Perceiving that you must have this job, you

117

must stay in this leadership position, you must get rid of that person or group in order to survive—will make it impossible for you to negotiate, both in terms of the fear that it will engender and in terms of the lack of flexibility of give and take. The reasoning seems to go, "If I don't get what I want I am dead. I am not getting what I want, I am dying."

Can you *change the definitions of the problem?* Often people bring a problem definition that puts you in a bad light or inhibits problem solving because of the way the problem is stated. For example, "You have not given us the training we need to do our job" implies that it is one person's responsibility to provide training. Other problem definitions might be, "The group has not sought the training it needs," or "The group has not had adequate training because funds are not available to get the training."

Another idea for the person under attack that deserves serious reflection is *give in on what is not important to you.* You don't have to win everything. In fact, you may have been doing some things incorrectly or inadequately. Nobody's perfect. Your willingness to show movement and to make some changes yourself that may be helpful to the entire organization will help get others to move as well. Resist the temptation to become rigid, petrified, frozen in the midst of challenges. I suppose nature has built into us human creatures the need to slow down, hold still, look things over when we are threatened, but this urge to conserve doesn't have to be absolute. Your changes will show that you can respond to others and give them a model for what they can do as well. In fact you can use your changing as a bargaining chip: "I'm changing; I'm doing things differently. How about you?"

As a rule of thumb, *meet with larger rather than smaller groups.* Expand the arena of participation. Individuals who represent or act for others tend to take more adamant stands, overstate their position (that is, the position of the faction or group). In representing others they tend to play to their audience outside the meeting rather than the audience across the table. If you get people participating, hearing, seeing, and involving themselves, the likelihood of getting them to join the team rather than to fight increases as they understand the big picture and all the implications involved.

Change turf. Sometimes a change in venue can help everyone look at things in a fresh way—especially if enough time has been allowed to work the problem in the new environment.

Ask for help. Bring in a third party. As I mentioned in the previous chapter, third parties can function as an unbiased audience, reminding people to be on their best behavior. Trusted third parties also are able to establish the processes and problem definitions that contenders won't allow each other to do. Further, helpers (whether they are actually helping you deal with the other person or persons or whether they are listening only to your side of the story) can assist you in getting a better perspective on yourself and the situation than may be the case if you were left to your own devices.

Conclusion

No matter what your particular role or experience in a given conflict may be—advoctate, defender, or third party—the same basic principle applies: conflict that is surfaced, addressed, and worked through can be productive for the total life of the organization. Conflict is

119

not managed by suppression or power plays. Further, you will be helped when dealing with differences if you keep in mind that two powerful dynamics are probably working in yourself and in others: the tension between the needs for dependence and independence and fear. Being aware of how fear is affecting you and how it is likely to be affecting others can help you develop strategies which decrease the tension and help everyone use their best selves for managing the conflict.

The next time you find yourself in a conflict, review those sections of the book that are relevant to your situation. This may help in a time of stress when emotions run high and intellectual efforts take special care. Analysis of your situation, using this book as a resource, can be an anxiety-reducing technique in itself. One way to start that analysis is to begin by outlining your "case" as you now understand it:

What were the triggering events?

Who is involved?

What do the various parties want or need?

What are the barriers to managing the conflict?

What is my role in the situation? Is it to be advocate, defender, or third party?

What steps can I take to invite others to deal with the differences?

After you have your perceptions on paper, review them in light of the material in the chapters that are relevant. Perhaps these chapters will give you other ideas and insights to deal with your situation. Good luck!

NOTES

Chapter I

1. Lewis Thomas, *The Lives of a Cell* (New York: Bantam Books, 1975), pp. 102, 104.
2. Stanley Milgram, *Obedience to Authority* (New York: Harper & Row, 1974).
3. *Ibid.*, p. 5.
4. Erich Fromm, *Beyond the Chains of Illusion: My Encounter with Marx and Freud* (New York: Simon & Schuster, 1962), p. 52.
5. James MacGregor Burns, *Leadership* (New York: Harper & Row, 1978), p. 117.

Chapter II

1. *Ibid.*, p. 18.
2. *Ibid.*, p. 20.
3. Rollo May, *Power and Innocence* (New York: W. W. Norton & Co., 1972), *passim.*
4. David C. McClelland, *Power: The Inner Experience* (New York: Halsted Press, 1975), p. 260.
5. Robert Tucker, "Theory of Charismatic Leadership," *Daedalus*, (Summer 1968), 749.

Chapter III

1. See especially Speed B. Leas and Paul L. Kittlaus, *Pastoral Care and Social Action* (Philadelphia: Fortress Press, 1980); Donald C. Klein, *Community Dynamics and Mental Health* (New York: John Wiley & Sons, 1968); *Church Planning* (Office of Church Life and Leadership, Church Leadership Resources, Box 179, St. Louis, Mo. 63166); Jack Fordyce and Raymond Weil, *Managing with People* (Reading, Ma.: Addison-Wesley Publishing Co., 1971).
2. Richard Gabriel and Paul Savage, *Crisis in Command* (New York: Hill & Wang, 1978).
3. *Ibid.*, pp. 160-61.
4. Adapted from the Influence Style Questionnaire, copyright Situation Management Systems, Inc., Box 476, Center Station, Plymouth, Ma. 02361.
5. Martin E. Seligman, *Helplessness: On Depression, Development, and Death* (San Francisco: W. H. Freeman & Co., 1975), p. 94.
6. I am indebted to David Berlew for these ideas from his article "Leadership and Organizational Excitement," *The California Management Review*, 2 (Winter 1974).
7. Glenna Joyce Holsinger, "Shaping Behavior with Reinforcement," *The Personnel Administrator*, (September-October 1972).

Chapter IV

1. Hans Selye, *Stress Without Distress* (Philadelphia: J. B. Lippincott Co., 1974), p. 39.
2. Richard Lazarus, "A Cognitively Oriented Psycholo-

gist Looks at Biofeedback," *The American Psychologist*, (1975), 553-61.

3. Colleen Kelly, *Assertion Training* (La Jolla, Ca.: University Associates, 1979), p. 139.

Chapter V

1. Stanley M. Herman and Michael Korenich, *Authentic Management* (Reading, Ma.: Addison-Wesley Publishing Co., 1977), pp. 57-58.
2. Adapted from George Bach and Herb Goldberg, *Creative Aggression* (New York: Avon Books, 1975).
3. Richard Bandler and John Grinder, *The Structure of Magic* (Palo Alto, Ca.: Science & Behavior Books, 1975), chapter 4.
4. John Scanzoni and Maximiliane Szinovacz, *Family Decision-Making* (Beverly Hills, Ca.: Sage Publications, 1980).
5. Jeffrey Rubin and Bert Brown, *The Social Psychology and Bargaining and Negotiation* (New York: Academic Press, 1975).

Chapter VI

1. William G. Dyer, *Team Building* (Reading, Ma.: Addison-Wesley Publishing Co., 1977), pp. 84-92.
2. Dayal and Thomas, "Operation KPE: Developing a New Organization," *Journal of Applied Behavioral Science*, (1968), 473-506.

Chapter VIII

1. P. G. Zimbardo, "Transforming Experimental Research Into Advocacy for Social Change," in *Applying Social Psychology: Implications for Research, Practice, and Training*, eds. Morton Deutsch and Harvey Hornstein (New York: Halsted Press, 1975).
2. Harvey Hornstein, *Cruelty and Kindness* (Englewood Cliffs, N. J.: Prentice-Hall, 1976), p. 140.